Carving Unreality - Volume 2

AF107596

OrangeBooks Publication

Smriti Nagar, Bhilai, Chhattisgarh - 490020

Website: **www.orangebooks.in**

© Copyright, 2022, Author

All rights reserved. No part of this book may be reproduced, stored in a retrieval system, or transmitted, in any form by any means, electronic, mechanical, magnetic, optical, chemical, manual, photocopying, recording or otherwise, without the prior written consent of its writer.

First Edition, 2022

ISBN: 978-93-5621-145-2

The opinions/ contents expressed in this book are solely of the author and do not represent the opinions/ standings/ thoughts of OrangeBooks.

CARVING UNREALITY

VOLUME 2

MUSTAFA MUN

OrangeBooks Publication
www.orangebooks.in

INDEX

Chapter-1 1

Chapter-2 9

Chapter-3 17

Chapter-4 25

Chapter-5 33

Chapter-6 41

Chapter-7 49

Chapter-8 57

Chapter-9 65

Chapter-10 73

Chapter-11 81

Chapter-12 90

Chapter-13 98

Chapter-14 106

CHAPTER-1

Kingston Interactive was ours. I remembered saying the words, but there was never a time before when I felt less like that was the case. Cole stood on the stage, speaking about the business, and so far he hadn't mentioned me once. Bringing me at all felt like a choice he'd made because he felt he had to. Had I not gone with him, people would have started asking questions he couldn't answer.

Every so often, I felt eyes on me. Did they wonder why I was there? How many of them knew I was the reason we were able to keep the company running? If they were taking Cole at face value, they'd assume I was only there for moral support, because he was my husband. The reality was very different.

Disappearing, leaving Cole to deal with his adoring fans, felt like the right thing to do, but I knew he wouldn't forgive me if I drew attention to myself right then. Sighing, I raked a hand through my hair, wishing there was another option. Instead, I sat there until everyone started politely clapping, telling me it was my chance to leave.

Standing, not looking at Cole, I walked down the aisle, focusing entirely on the door. Someone reached it before I did, and they held it open for me. I didn't even look at who it was. I just walked through the door, feeling the first of the tears beginning to prickle at the backs of my eyes, making it very obvious that I needed to get far away before I made a spectacle of myself. That was another thing he wouldn't forgive.

The man I loved was gone. He'd been taken over by the CEO of Kingston Interactive, forgetting how much of myself I'd put into the company. Stepping into the bathroom, I barely made it to one of the stalls before the tears started falling, and it was then I realised someone was following me, which was exactly what I didn't need, at least until I realised who it was.

Katie wrapped her arms around me, letting me sob into her shoulder as she closed the door with a foot. The last thing I wanted to do was be seen when I was in that kind of state, but I had made a terrible decision—I'd left my bag behind, not thinking about it, because all I'd wanted to do was get away.

"I'm sorry, Lou."

"So am I." I breathed in deeply, trying to calm my emotions, my eyes meeting hers for a moment. "How bad do I look?"

"You're doing a very good impression of a panda."

"Great."

"What do you need?"

"My bag. I left it in the main room."

"Okay, I can do that." She pulled some tissues out of her bag for me, holding them out, and I accepted them, needing them more than I realised. "I won't be long."

"Thank you."

"Being there for a friend is the more important thing."

***

Cole's eyes met with mine. "Where were you?"

"Getting coffee with a friend." It seemed like mentioning the friend's name was going to cause more problems than it solved. "You didn't seem to need me."

"Lou..."

"How are you going to explain it away this time?" I studied him, seeing the annoyance in his eyes because he cared far more about appearances than anything else. "I was sitting right there, Cole, listening to you talk about Kingston Interactive as though I had nothing to do with it."

"They wanted me to talk about the headsets."

"No, you wanted to talk about the headsets. They wanted you to talk about Kingston Interactive, which is far more than just the headsets, and we both know we wouldn't be where we are if it weren't for the time I put into the games we're selling".

For a few seconds, he was silent. His silence didn't mean he was thinking about what I said. We'd had the same argument so many times before, and we still hadn't gotten anywhere. Cole still wasn't willing to accept how important I was to Kingston, something I was more than a little tired of, especially since I knew he wouldn't be where he was without me.

Both of us put in hours to get to where we were. I was the one who brought in the money early on and kept bringing in the money with the games. People liked the headsets, but they wouldn't have bought them without the games, meaning we had two different sides to the business. The academic side was something we still worked on together, while the games were mine. Cole still didn't see any reason to waste time on them.

"Maybe it would be better for you not to come to these talks." Cole stepped away from me. "If you're going to get emotional, then there's no reason for you to be there. This is about business, nothing more".

"Yes, it is, and I am a part of that business, Cole. I'm only a part you never talk about. Anyone sitting there wouldn't know I had anything to do with Kingston Interactive. I think it would be better for me not to come to those talks. After today, I also think it would be better for me to step away from Kingston Interactive entirely".

"If that's what you want, Lou, I'm not going to talk you out of it." He shrugged. "You can take a couple of weeks off, work through what it is you want to do next, and then come back when you're feeling more capable of being logical."

Blinking, I stared at him, wishing I knew why he thought the words I said meant I wanted a holiday. It wasn't something I was going to argue about. A couple of weeks was enough time for me to make a plan as to what my next steps were going to be. More than anything, I wanted to take my intellectual property with me, but that might end up being something I gave to Kingston Interactive, rather than fighting Cole for it.

Saying anything seemed like it was only going to cause more problems. I headed for my office, somewhere I could work alone because there was no reason for me to put anything off. He'd made his decision. Cole didn't see me as an integral part of Kingston Interactive. If he did, he'd have mentioned me at least once.

Dropping into my chair, breathing in deeply, I turned on my PC. Once I'd logged into my email, I wasn't surprised to see something from Katie, checking in on me again. She was the one who knew the most about my problems with Cole. Talking to her was easier than it was to anyone else because she understood things other people might not have.

Without really thinking about it I set up a call with her. "I'm okay".

"Really?"

"Cole's made a decision, and now I need to make mine."

"Have you got any idea what that might be?"

"Yes, I have, but it's not something I think I should talk about right now. I need to sleep on it. I'm emotional, Kate, and that's not a time to make any decisions".

"Today you're emotional. Last week you weren't. I know how unhappy you are, Lou, and you have been for a while. This... I don't want to tell you what you should be doing, but this isn't the first time he's done this to you".

***

Sleeping in the same bed wasn't something we'd done for a long time. I'd set myself up a space in my office for the nights when I most wanted to be away from Cole, and in a lot of ways, it was more comfortable. Laying there, staring up at the ceiling, I curled my arms around myself, remembering the nights when Cole used to be the one doing that.

Those memories were the most painful ones. No matter what I did I couldn't free myself of them. Leaving Kingston Interactive meant leaving the man I loved. The man who'd been such an important part of my life for so long. I felt the tears prickling once more. As things fell apart, I'd find myself crying more and more often, because I knew we couldn't keep going the way we were.

Cole, of course, would say I was being illogical, letting my emotions get in the way of making the best choices I could. We should be putting Kingston first, not anything else. Especially not our relationship. For now, the company is more important than anything else. He'd said those words to me so many times that I should have left long before I did.

Rolling onto my side, almost certain it was going to be another night where I wouldn't get any sleep, I raked a hand through my hair. Maybe I shouldn't give it two weeks. There were plenty of people I knew who would take me in until I could get myself sorted. Being in a house with Cole for that long was going to cause far more problems than it could possibly solve.

Breathing in deeply, I closed my eyes. I didn't feel tired. Not physically tired. I was emotionally tired, yes, but that wasn't enough to make me sleep. Slipping out from under the blanket, certain Cole would be in his office, I made my way into the bedroom, finding one of my suitcases.

Gathering clothes, not really caring what they were, I shoved them in, doing my best to take as much as I could in one go. It wasn't something Cole would notice. I didn't really think he paid that much attention to me anymore. There had been points where I'd tried to date him again, the romance in our relationship dead, but it didn't work. For us to have a relationship he needed to put some effort in.

For us to be able to work together he needed to put some effort in. All he cared about were the people he could impress by being the CEO of Kingston Interactive, and I wasn't one of them. Not when I was the COO, the CFO, and the CCO. I wore far more hats than he could imagine, making things far harder for him than it would be for me if I did walk away.

I had plans for new games, some I'd chosen to hold back because it made more sense to keep them to myself. Adding them to the Kingston Interactive roster would likely end with me losing them, and that wasn't something I wanted. Not with those. They were something I could use to make my own income, build up my own business, and maybe even turn to Katie. She said her offer wasn't a one-time thing.

Everything together, my suitcase as full as I was going to make it, I headed back into the office, packing up my laptop and my notes. The PC itself was locked. No one could get on it without me, and there was no chance of Cole guessing my password now. Once, he'd have been able to easily. Now I was a stranger to him, a woman he no longer knew anything about, because he'd walked away from everything, without ever seeing his choices as the wrong ones.

He didn't notice as I left the house, making my way to the car. Putting the suitcase into the back I thought about where to go, and I knew there was one person who'd help me out no matter what. Starting the engine, wondering if that would be enough to draw his attention, I reversed out of the drive. Even though I shouldn't have done it, I looked back.

No sign of my husband. He was gone. Cole have believed he was still the man who loved me, but his actions said something else entirely. All I needed to do was accept it. I couldn't go back in the morning and pretend everything was okay. Everything wasn't okay. Everything was never going to be okay.

CHAPTER-2

Knocking on Sarah's door so late wasn't something I was happy doing, but she was the only person I could think of who'd be willing to let me in if I turned up on the doorstep with a suitcase in my hand. There was a chance she wouldn't hear me because I knew Alex rose early, and if she didn't, then I'd go to a hotel.

Seconds later, I thought I heard footsteps. When the door opened, Sarah was confused on the other side; I realised I had no idea what to say. How do I tell her now after all the time I'd spent pretending everything was fine. But everything wasn't fine, and I desperately needed a place to stay that was away from Cole.

Fortunately, she didn't ask any questions straight away. Instead, she stepped back, letting me in, and as she closed the door, I felt the tears streaming down my cheeks again. Curling an arm around my shoulders, holding me tight, Sarah took me into the kitchen. There she turned the light on, going straight to the fridge. The hot chocolate was a necessity right then. Talking about Cole… I breathed in deeply, dropping my suitcase on the floor.

"I'm sorry."

"What's happened?"

"Cole…" I raked a hand through my hair, trying to find the words. "I don't know where to start. Things have been hard."

"Kingston Interactive?"

Nodding slowly, more tears escaping, I bit down on my bottom lip. "It's been… complicated."

"Alex has been keeping me up to date. We've seen a couple of the talks, Lou". Sarah looked at me for a moment, before putting the milk on the hob. "Cole hasn't mentioned you at any of them so far."

"No, he hasn't." I breathed in deeply, wiping the tears off my cheeks, only for them to be replaced in seconds. "Apparently my work doesn't matter, even though I'm the one who's kept things going. Without the money I was bringing in, we wouldn't have Kingston Interactive." I shook my head. "Talking about it… I don't know. Sometimes it felt like bringing this up with you, with how long you've been a part of our lives, made it real."

Glancing back at me, nodding, Sarah got mugs out of the cupboard, getting the biggest ones I think she owned. "I get it. Coming here means it's over?"

Unable to bring myself to say the words I looked down at the floor. "I don't know. It should be. Cole… he's not the man I fell in love with, Sarah, and that… being around him is hard. I've tried to talk to him about this so many times, only to have him tell me I need to be more logical. He believes he's doing what's best for the company."

"Only focusing on the company means he's not doing what's best for the two of you. Your relationship is one of the most important things, because without that there is no Kingston Interactive, although it seems like he's entirely forgotten about that element."

"He has." I ran my tongue over my bottom lip. "I never thought this was how things were going to fall apart. Back when we were struggling, and the company was taking all of our spare time, I could see it happening, but this… well, it is what it is. There's nothing I can do to change him, is there? I knew how much Kingston meant to him."

"Kingston shouldn't mean more to him than you do." Sarah stirred the milk into the mugs, before going back over to the fridge. "The two of you are the bedrock of Kingston, with you having the knowledge to make an income even before his element of the business was up and running, so the decision to shut you out is going to end up destroying everything he's worked toward."

"Do I leave?" I looked at Sarah, as she added the cream on top, a sign of how bad she thought things were. "I need someone to tell me it's okay."

"Lou, of course, it's okay." She put one of the mugs in front of me. "You shouldn't stay with him if you aren't happy. He's been the one talking about logical choices, and staying with someone who isn't acting like he loves you sounds like the least logical thing anyone could possibly do."

***

I was on the laptop when Alex came down the stairs. Sarah, I hoped, told him I was there, so it wasn't too much of a surprise. He gave me a smile, before heading for the kitchen. "You want a coffee, Lou?"

"No, I'm good, thanks." I scrolled down the page of properties to rent, thinking about what I wanted. "I'm sorry for being here."

"Don't apologise. We're your friends, and this is exactly where you should be." Alex sighed. "I'm sorry Cole's being a fool." There was a moment of silence, and I heard him making coffee. "You've kept in contact with the people who were your friends before Kingston Interactive started taking off. No one has heard from Cole in about six months."

"Really?" I bit down on my bottom lip. "I didn't know he was shutting everyone out."

"Life changes, and I get that. He's busy, but so are you, and the way he's acting makes it obvious none of us matter anymore. Cole wasn't someone I could see doing that until it happened. Watching the talks... Sarah and I did want to bring it up before, but she said it was probably better to wait until you were ready to talk to us."

Alex stepped into the living room, mug in his hands. "Honestly, I should have talked to you a long time ago." I breathed in deeply. "Like I said to Sarah last night having that conversation with you made it too real. Being here, talking to the two of you about how our relationship has slowly died, means I have to move on. I have to make the logical choices, rather than cling on to something that no longer exists."

"Have you thought about the next steps?"

"Yes, but that's something I need to talk to a lawyer about. I'm prepared to give up certain elements of my IP to Kingston Interactive if it means we can have a clean break."

He studied me. "Do you think Cole cares?" I blinked. "He never talks about your side of the business. I've noticed his concentration in one of the headsets and in the Virtual School. Understandable, because it's his side of the business, but the majority of the money is still being brought in by the gaming side of Kingston Interactive. From the way he speaks, I don't think he understands how important it is. You are the foundation of the business."

"We both are."

"Be honest with yourself, Lou. If Cole was on his own, do you really believe he would have been able to get to where he is?"

"Possibly not."

Laughing, he shook his head. "Go over the numbers. Not that I think you need to, because you know them better than he does, but check them, and then tell yourself you aren't the reason Kingston's still going. I don't even need to look at them to know for certain he wouldn't have a business without you."

***

Even though Alex was right, I did already know, I still went over the numbers, to track everything. If I went to Cole and asked him to split the business, I had to be logical about it. Would he be willing to give up the most profitable element of the business, simply because he didn't believe it mattered? I breathed in deeply, starting to write down notes.

More than anything, I did want my IP back. Had I known things were going to work out the way they had I wouldn't have tied them to Kingston Interactive in the first place. Running my tongue over my bottom lip, thinking about Katie again, I knew she was someone I should talk to. She was still funding my side of the company, and I needed details on what might happen if that were to happen.

Giving in to the urge, in part because it would be helpful moving forward, I drew the laptop closer to me and started typing out the email. Katie probably already knew it was coming, after what happened at the talk. She'd been trying to convince me to leave Cole for at least a couple of months, having seen what he was doing at all the talks he gave, telling me I was letting my emotions get in the way of making the more logical choices.

It was seconds after I sent it that I got the request for a call, and I answered it, grabbing my headset as I did. "Hi, Katie."

"Okay, how hypothetical is the question?"

"For now, assume entirely." I breathed in deeply. "It's likely that I am going to leave, but I'm still not certain. Before I can make any definite decisions, I need to talk to Cole, and see what he's willing to do, although I am willing to give up any IP I worked on that's currently under the Kingston Interactive name. "

"You shouldn't, but I can understand why you would. Having a clean break is more important." I could hear her drawing papers toward her. "I remember you speaking before of other plans you were making, that I haven't yet seen come to fruition, which I'm assuming is due to the issues you've been having with Cole."

"They are. When I realised the situation, I'd found myself in, the only games I put out were related to the series I'd started before. I do have plenty of options when it comes to new games I can bring out once I've left Kingston, but I need to leave first. One of my friends, Alex, doesn't think Cole will be interested in keeping the games, which might well be the case."

"Cole believes, and has done since we first started talking, that Kingston Interactive could rely on the headsets, with the Virtual School, for the majority of their income. The two of us know that's not the case, so it is possible he will give up that IP. However, it's not something I'd rely on if you are going to move forward. How about we talk about what you might be able to do when you have left?"

"Okay, I have three games fully ready to go, each of them a new IP. Cole doesn't know they exist, because we never talk about anything anymore. I have two more in progress, and they won't take much longer to get done, as we're close to the testing phase." I bit down on my bottom lip. "Before he made the decision, we didn't need you as an investor we did talk about bringing in someone else, but after he acted as though it wasn't a conversation we'd had."

"Another sign your friends might be right. Does he honestly believe in the gaming side of the business, does he?"

"No, he saw it as a distraction rather than anything else. To him, the most important part was getting the headsets out, and the Virtual School running, not seeing how we needed the money to be able to make that happen before we had investors. Even with them, it wasn't enough. Looking at the numbers today, if I were to pull out, with all my IP, it's likely Kingston Interactive would fail within the year. Of course, that's something I don't think Cole understands."

"He doesn't look at the numbers himself?"

"Why would he? I've taken on the task of dealing with the finances. I did try to get him to look, but I gave up in the end."

CHAPTER-3

Calling Cole was one of the strangest experiences. I raked a hand through my hair, waiting for him to answer, only to get sent to his voicemail. "When you have a chance to talk, call me back."

Rather than waiting for it to happen, because it was entirely possible, he wouldn't, I turned my attention to the apartment in front of me. I'd planned to meet the Realtor to look around, knowing I wasn't going back to Cole. I hadn't heard from him, even via email, so I didn't know if he'd noticed I'd basically moved out.

Slipping out of the car, breathing in deeply, I started walking toward the building. Did I really want to live in an apartment? Financially, it made the most sense. Get somewhere small, and then move up later on when I was certain things were going to work out. There was no way of knowing if people were actually going to follow me if I started a new company.

Katie believed they would. Even though Cole never mentioned my name at the talks he gave, people knew I was the game developer if they had any interest in the games. I'd seen it all over the Internet, which was kind of nice, but that did mean I also saw some of the darker side, and the reason people didn't know until the right time that Katie was the person behind Patterson.

The Realtor waited for me by the door. He gave me a smile. "Mrs. Kingston." He held his hand out, and I shook it. "I believe you're here to see one of the two-bedroom apartments."

Nodding, I raked a hand through my hair. "I am."

"Is this a new home for your family?"

"Unfortunately, not." I didn't go into details, because he didn't need to know. "I'm going to need the second bedroom for an office because I work from home."

Hearing that seemed to make him cool a little, gesturing for me to follow him. "What do you do?"

Did it matter? I know, logically, he was only trying to make conversation, and I'd shut him down during the family conversation. Bringing up Cole right then really wasn't something I wanted to do. "I'm a game developer."

Glancing back at me, cooling a little more, he nodded. "Make anything I might know?"

"Maybe. It depends on what kind of games you're interested in." I shrugged. "Do you know much about Kingston Interactive?"

Again, he glanced back at me, this time seeming confused. "I know about their headsets. I see Cole Kingston talking about them all the time, along with the Virtual School. My son's school is actually talking to him about getting some of them because they think it would be useful for certain classes."

I smiled. "Some of the work we've done to build up the history and geography classes has been amazing. I think your son's school would get a lot of use out of them."

***

After dialling Cole's number again, after giving him eight hours to call me back, I bit down on my bottom lip. I didn't think he was going to answer. He was probably too busy, or at least that was what he told himself. Honestly, I doubted he even looked at the phone before he made the decision not to answer it, because if he did, he was going to need to take a time out.

When I went through voicemail again, I didn't bother to leave another message. He probably hadn't heard the one I left. If he had, he might have called back, although I had a feeling he didn't care enough to bother. Sighing, I raked a hand through my hair, tossing my phone to one side. Obviously, the only logical thing I could do was email him, in the hope he might see that. That was actually more likely to get through to him, because that was something he checked regularly, in case one of the investors needed something.

Finding the right words was the hardest thing to do. Breathing in deeply, emotions swirling, I knew I needed to keep things logical. Talking about our marriage in the same email as I talked about the company would probably lead to Cole ignoring it. However, our marriage was on the rocks, the same way our business relationship was.

After an hour of work, carefully crafting an email that told him everything he needed to know, I sent it, wondering if it might get me a response. I laid out the terms I was hoping for, so we could work from there. Cole might not be willing to give up my IP if he talked to someone before he made the decision, but there was a chance he wouldn't bother. Even though it was a stupid decision to make I wasn't going to tell him to talk to a lawyer. It was something he should have known to do.

Sending it took a weight off my shoulders in a way I hadn't imagined it could. Leaving Kingston Interactive was the first step. Once we'd done that, I could think about divorce. Dealing with the business first seemed like the most logical option, especially as there was a chance not working together would have a good effect on our personal relationship.

I stood, leaving the room I was borrowing from Sarah's, thinking about what to do for food. Having randomly turned up, I didn't want to make life harder for the two of them, so getting a takeaway probably made the most sense. It wasn't as though I hadn't been living off of them, and frozen meals, because there was no logical reason for me to put in the effort to cook for myself alone.

Reaching the kitchen, where Sarah was already cooking, I saw a third plate on the counter. "Sarah..."

"You deserve to have someone look after you for a little while, Lou." She glanced back at me. "Is Cottage Pie good for you?"

Having an evening with two people who actually cared about me was nice. It reminded me of how different my relationship with Cole had been before we started building Kingston Interactive. During the early days it was difficult because I didn't know if I could be a part of the company, to begin with, and then when I did start working toward that goal, he still wasn't happy. I'd made a decision he didn't agree with, as he was entirely focused on the headsets even then.

Before that, when we didn't have dual elements to our relationship, we'd been happier, or I thought we were. Maybe I'd simply had on rose-tinted glasses, seeing things the way I wanted to, rather than how they were. He was still the kind of person who'd take over sometimes, something I thought we'd worked through before our marriage. What I wanted was for us to be equals.

My phone rang, and I glanced at it. Cole was finally calling me. I breathed in deeply, settling my emotions before I answered the call. "Cole."

"What is that email about?"

Sighing, I raised an eyebrow. "I thought it was relatively self-explanatorily."

"Lou…"

"You believed I only wanted to take some time away from the company, to work through some issues. That's not what I was saying from the beginning. I always planned on leaving Kingston Interactive. You may think otherwise, but this is something that's been going through my head for a while now, and this…" I bit down on my bottom lip. "We aren't working together. I don't think we have for a long time."

"Kingston Interactive is our company, Louise."

"No, it's your company. You've made that much clear. I know you don't think that's what you've done. Unfortunately, what you think doesn't matter, because it's how you've been treating me that's led to this."

"Does this have something to do with the talks?"

"Of course, it does, but it's more than the talk. It's how you've treated me the entire time we've been working together. The headsets have been your focus since the beginning, which is something I understand because it is an important element. However, as important as that is, we wouldn't be where we are without the work I've done, and yet it's not something that seems to matter to you."

For a few seconds, Cole was silent. "It matters. You matter."

"Unfortunately, I've given you multiple chances to prove that to me, and you haven't. I know you think we might be able to move forward together if you say what you think I want to hear, but that's not what's going to happen this time. You've said the words more than once when

I've told you how I feel. Only it's never been enough to get you to understand the damage you've done to our business relationship, along with our personal one, so it's gotten to the point where I believe the only option, I have is to leave Kingston."

"Take a couple of nights to think about this."

"Cole, I can't think about it any more than I already have done. I'm leaving Kingston Interactive. Exactly how it works depends on you. If you think we can move forward amicably, then that will help, because I don't want this to be hard for either of us. I need something else, something better, where I feel happy again.

"All I feel right now is unhappy. I don't feel like what I do matters to you, or to Kingston. You are Kingston. We've been working on the company together, but you're the one who's been working with all the investors, as though I don't exist. I think, now, it would be easier for both of us if I didn't."

"Okay, how about we get together? Spend a night talking through plans? I can see why you feel the way you do. My focus has been on the headsets, because they're one of the most important elements of the business, and it means I've made mistakes. That doesn't end with us splitting the company into two. It can't."

"Yes, it can. I don't know how talking about this is going to change anything. You'll be attentive to my needs for a week, maybe, if I'm lucky, and then things will go back to how they were. It's what happened before, Cole. We've had this same conversation multiple times, only for me to find it doesn't matter because you go back to normal in barely any time at all.

"The first time it happened I believed you could change. After several attempts, I'm past that. You can't change it. I'm not falling for the words this time. If you want to show me, I mean something to you and give our personal relationship a chance to go back to normal, then you have to let me leave Kingston."

Silence followed my words again. "Do you really think we can have a personal relationship if you leave Kingston?"

"Honestly, I don't know. I'm not willing to pretend. This might be the end of everything, but if it is then maybe it was meant to be. I need a different life, one where I feel I matter to someone, and I don't think you're ever going to be able to make me feel like that when you're so focused on Kingston."

"Meaning you're willing to give up everything we have."

"Yes, I am." Giving in to his manipulations was something I'd done before because I didn't want to give up on everything, but if that was the only way things could be then so be it. "Our relationship might have a chance if we can find a way through this. If you can find a way through this. When it comes to Kingston, I'm not making an emotional decision. I'm making a logical one. You should do the same thing, rather than letting anything else get in the way."

CHAPTER-4

Cole sat at the table, a cup of coffee already in front of him. I glanced at the counter, thinking about options, before going straight over to him, not wanting the meeting to end up lasting longer than it needed to. When he saw I didn't have anything he studied me. I knew him. He thought the meeting was going to be a chance for him to talk me out of making a decision he thought was wrong.

"Let me get you something."

"No, thank you." I breathed in deeply as I dropped into the seat opposite him. "All I'm here to do is talk about Kingston Interactive, and how we're going to split the company."

For a moment, I could see the emotion in his eyes, making him look like the Cole I fell in love with, and then it was gone like it hadn't existed at all. "Do you believe you've put in the work to split the company in half?"

"Yes, I do."

Pulling out some papers that had probably been on the seat beside him, he put them on the table in front of me. "This is what my lawyer has drafted, with the information I've given him about the company."

I read through the contract slowly, taking in the words one at a time, and it was all I could do to keep from laughing. "I'm assuming you didn't show your lawyer the income split between the two elements of Kingston Interactive." Taking two different contracts out of my bag, knowing they were the fairer ones, I put them on the table in front of him. "I've gone through all the finances, and this is a fair split between us, considering how much of the income comes from the games.

"The first is if you give me my intellectual property back, so I can move forward with the series, but the second exists if you aren't willing to do that." I studied him, seeing no emotion at all, although I didn't think he'd expected me to be prepared, almost like he'd never met me. "Please let me know which one of the two you prefer."

"We will be going with my contract."

"In that case, I'll see you in court."

Blinking, he stared at me, as I put his contract into my bag. "What do you mean?"

"Exactly what I said. If you push your contract, then I'll be going to court to get a fair split. I suggest you show the contracts to your lawyer, and then make a decision."

Grabbing my bag, I stood, walking away from the table before Cole could say anything more. I had a feeling he was going to try that, which was why I had prepared for it. Stepping out into the air, feeling a slight breeze on my face, I started walking away from the coffee shop, hoping he wasn't going to follow me. It seemed unlikely. He believed I was going to give him what he wanted, and I'd shown him otherwise.

***

Katie laughed. "Your husband is a moron."

"I know." I shrugged. "He made his choices, and now he's going to have to live with them."

"His lawyer can't have known the whole situation with the finances of the company, otherwise he wouldn't have written something so unfair. The two you gave Cole are far fairer. Personally, I'd be willing to fight for your IP, but I can understand why you want a clean break after everything you've been through up to this point."

"Giving him control over them isn't something I want to do. He doesn't know the plans I had for any of them, and I hate the thought of them being abandoned by Kingston Interactive, because I'm certain that's what he'll do given a chance, so… yeah. I think if I wasn't so tired right now, I might have fought, but as it is I can't bring myself to put the energy in."

"We can talk about your plans away from Kingston."

Smiling, I nodded. "I'd have a company up and running by now, if I'd made a decision on the name, I wanted to give it a go, as that, for now, seems to be the hardest part."

"Okay, let's go over the ideas you have."

"For now, the plan is to focus purely on the game series I have already planned out. I do have two different timelines set out, depending on whether I get the IP back from Kingston Interactive. Having them up will mean people will know who I am sooner, but I feel I've built up a good following as a game developer, and they'll follow me even if it means buying different IPs." I ran my tongue over my bottom lip. "That being the case I want to take a step back from using my name in the company name."

"Unfortunately, that's pretty much as far as I've got. I don't know what name makes the most sense, even though I've been scribbling down ideas for days. Some of the names are already taken by other companies, who do very different things, and I hate naming things."

Grinning, Katie shook her head. "Why is it you think I went for my name? Coming up with a name is one of the hardest parts, especially when you want to draw people in." She drew a piece of paper toward her. "What do you want people to think when they hear your name?"

"Being one of the main issues I've had. I don't know what I want people to think. I could go for a fun name, but I don't know if that's what I want to do. Obviously, going for something linked to Kingston is out, because I don't want it to be linked at all to Cole's company, so maybe I could go for something linked to being solo now."

Nodding, she fell silent, and I watched her scribbling things down. "There are a lot of terrible ideas that I had to get out of my head before I could start with the logical ones. I didn't want to go for anything linked to the IPs Kingston might keep control of either, which is something I'm also certain you thought about, but I kept coming back to using Diamond in the name. Obviously, that's because I think of you as a diamond." Katie looked at me, her eyes meeting mine for a moment. "Lone Diamond, maybe?"

"Or Blue Diamond? Something along those lines." I typed the name into a search. "Any crystal might work, though. Sapphire Studios." She tilted her head to one side, writing down more ideas. "Amethyst Studios?" She bit down on her bottom lip. "Constant Amethyst?"

"Hence the problem I've been having." I smiled at her, as she looked at me. Her eyes met mine. "Fortunately, I have a bit of time before I need a name, and then I can move on from there. Already having games ready to go does make this easier. There are a couple of others I've been working on over the last few days, trying to get things finished off, and making plans for the next ones in the series."

"You're right there, and it might be best to wait to get this done until you're entirely free of Kingston Interactive."

"A potential divorce also makes it complicated."

"True." Katie nodded. "You could become a part of my company if it would make things easier."

***

Not knowing exactly what was going to happen with Kingston Interactive, we started working through options for both. Katie wanted me to work with her, taking on the position of CCO, and building up a new side of her company. We'd started working out names, although that was something we hadn't made a decision on.

While I shared the potential plan for the different series with her, she started working on an announcement to share with the world when I was done with Kingston Interactive. Both of us were happy with a contract that said I would keep full control over my IP if the time came when we could no longer work together.

As it was, I didn't see any issues. From experience, I knew that Katie was already an easier person to work with than Cole. Of course, that was still something Cole knew nothing about because he'd made the decision that he didn't want anything to do with Patterson, but without their supporting the work I was doing, we definitely wouldn't have got as far as we had. Having the money coming in gave me the freedom to do more with the games than I had done before.

Had Cole been willing to work with me on that side of the business things would have ended up being very different. Instead, he shut me down, acting as though nothing I did mattered, which was one of the many reasons I needed to leave Kingston. Katie was the one I could talk to, and we bounced ideas around more than once to get me through a minor block, something I would always appreciate.

I went through the spreadsheet again, double-checking the games I had ready to go, the games I had close to being ready, and the games I wanted to work on: I had a very long list. Fortunately, I had multiple good artists I'd been working with, who had worked purely with me. If Cole did want to continue with my old IP, he'd have to build up a relationship with them, unless he wanted to go for something different, which likely wouldn't go well for him.

I shook my head at myself. Thinking about Cole all the time would get me nowhere. It seemed to be all I did. I bit down on my bottom lip, and as I did my phone rang. I sighed. Looking at it, seeing Cole's name, I sighed. Of course, he was going to call me right when I told myself to stop thinking about him.

"Cole."

"Louise." He breathed it in deeply. "I've spoken to my lawyer, and he went through the contracts you left with me, before asking to see why you believed they were fairer than the contract he wrote. He wasn't pleased with the decision I made to not give him all the information he needed, although it wasn't the information, I believed he needed at the time."

Raising an eyebrow, grateful he couldn't see my expression, I ran my tongue over my bottom lip. "How would you like to move forward?"

"Due to Kingston Interactive not having any plans moving forward to continue with that side of the business, I've made the decision it would be best for me to go with the contract which gives you full control over that. I know there are people who'd be very upset if they were abandoned completely.

"Going to court wouldn't be in Kingston Interactive's best interest, as it would cost a lot to deal with this when we can do it easily with a contract. When would you be willing to get together with our lawyers to sign the contract? I know you want to get this done sooner rather than later because I'm certain you have plans to move forward."

"Yes, I do." I checked my schedule. "I believe I can do it by Friday if that works for you."

"Friday works fine. I'll see you then."

Hanging up without saying goodbye wasn't something Cole had done in the past, but he obviously wasn't happy with me for the choices I'd made. First, he thought he was going to be able to talk me into staying, then he thought he could manipulate me into giving up more than I should, and in doing so he'd shown his true colours. Fortunately, this would mean everything was disconnected when it came to the business, making the divorce much easier. Hopefully. I could just see him attempting the same manipulations.

CHAPTER-5

Signing the contract was more tense than I expected it to be. Cole wasn't happy; he wasn't looking at me at all, and I had hoped we might be able to have a conversation about what both of us wanted from our personal relationship. Instead, he shut me out. The way he acted told me everything I needed to know. Now that I'd stepped away from Kingston Interactive it freed us both.

Watching him leave, almost certain any relationship we might have had was dead, I raked a hand through my hair. "Thank you both for the time you've put into this." I looked between the two lawyers. "I'm sorry for the problems you had with Cole not giving you all the information you needed to be able to write a fair contract."

"Unfortunately, it's not unheard of. Attempting it on you seems to have been the true mistake he made." He held his hand out, and I shook it. "Good luck with the future, Mrs. Kingston."

Leaving with my lawyer, grateful it was over, I headed to my car, thinking about the next steps. I had my copy of the contract, and my lawyer had another in case anything happened to it, so it was time to move away from Kingston Interactive entirely. There was so much I'd been putting off, not wanting it to belong to Kingston, but maybe it hadn't been necessary with how things had worked out eventually.

At the time, it seemed like the most logical choice. The other thing I needed, for when I moved into my new apartment, was my PC. Calling Cole to get that didn't seem like it was going to be the easiest thing to do, but I did still have my key. The house was still part mine, so I was able to walk in to get whatever I wanted, although it was possible, he might have changed the locks. If he did, I'd still be able to get what I needed, because he didn't have the right to lock me out.

It was an emotional choice, but I knew it was the right decision to make, and I headed toward the house I'd once called home. When I reached it, Cole's car wasn't there. Breathing a sigh of relief because it would make things easier, I got out of the car, and headed for the front door. As I put the key into the door all I could do was hope I'd be able to unlock it.

Gratefully I could, probably because up until the signing Cole still thought he'd be able to talk me out of leaving the company. I headed to my office, to find that the door was open. I hadn't left it open. Stepping into the room, my heart sinking, I stared at what had been my PC. I pulled my phone out of my pocket and took pictures of it.

Fortunately, I had backups of everything I'd been working on, in multiple different places.

My USBs were fine. I took the collection of them out of the drawer, shaking my head as I did. They went into my pocket, and then I left the house again, not closing the door. If things went the way I hoped they would, Cole wouldn't know I was there. Of course, it did mean I needed to buy a new PC. At least I had money set aside for that.

Getting in the car, I gave myself a moment to work through my emotions. Cole was so angry with me that he'd destroyed my PC. Having the proof at least meant I could make him pay for it, because he'd damaged something of mine, and that wasn't something I was going to accept. The man I'd fallen in love with would never do something like that. He'd never been violent, but maybe when he realised, he couldn't get to my work, he made the decision he'd simply give it to me.

As I drove back to Sarah's, where I was going to be for another week, I worked through what I might say to Cole about my PC because it was something we needed to talk about. Unfortunately, it was too late for me to get it back, after I'd spent time customizing it to my specifications, because of how much time I had spent working on the game.

Pulling onto the drive, in the spot they'd given me, I finally let myself cry. It was over. There was no doubt in my mind. A divorce was the next logical step, with Kingston Interactive dealt with, and it was going to happen even if Cole hadn't destroyed my PC. That was simply a sign of who the man I loved had become in the time we'd been working to build the company.

***

"Are you okay?"

Of course, Sarah knew the moment she saw me that there was something wrong. We'd known each other too long for her to miss it. "The Contract's signed, and I made the decision I'd grab my PC from the house before anything could happen to it. Unfortunately, it seems to have been something I should have taken with me when I first left."

Sarah stared at me. She knew Cole almost as well as I did, and the thought of him doing something to damage my property was one she'd never had either. Why would she? Our marriage had been mostly good until Kingston changed our lives, but that was a decision we'd made together. From the beginning, we knew there was a chance that things might fall apart, even though we both hoped it wouldn't.

Cole becoming someone entirely different wasn't something I could have imagined until it happened. "I'm so sorry. This..." She shook her head. "He's changed more than I could have imagined, Lou."

"Yeah, I know." I raked my hand through my hair. "With Kingston sorted I'll aim to move out soon. I think it would be better for all of us. The last thing I want is for anything to happen to you and Alex."

"Do you really think that might happen?"

"I wish I could say I knew. The man I fell in love with would never have harmed my PC." I pulled my phone out of my pocket, and scrolling to the pictures, which I held out to Sarah. "Cole did that."

Taking the phone Sarah went through the pictures I'd taken, shaking her head as she did. "How did he become the kind of person who could do something like this?"

"Anger, sometimes, gets the better of people, however calm they might be normally. I can only assume this was one of those times, but it is something I'm going to need to talk to him about. Even if I hadn't seen it then we'd have needed to have a conversation, and I want to see if he tells me what he did. If not, then he really has become someone I can't trust."

Giving me the phone back, fortunately with the gallery closed, I locked it and slipped it back into my pocket. "Let me know if you need anything, Lou. I also would like to know how that conversation goes, in case there are any issues we might need to be aware of because that…" She shook her head again. "I don't know what to say."

"One moment of anger I can forgive, in time. If it was anything more than that I'll talk to you about what we might need to do next, because the last thing I wanted was for you to have to deal with this."

Dialling Cole's number wasn't the easiest thing for me to do. The likelihood of him answering was low, but it was worth a try. If he didn't then I could send him an email, because that might get him to call me, the way it had before. I leaned against the wall, waiting to see if he was going to answer.

"Louise."

"Cole." I ran my tongue over my bottom lip, trying to find the words I needed. "As I'm going to be working elsewhere, I'll need access to the house to get my PC back."

Silence followed my words. I waited for him to say something because I wasn't going to be the one to break it, and then he sighed. I'm sorry, but that's not going to be possible. What I can do, however, is give you money for a new PC, as I erroneously purchased one. I don't want to talk too much about what I need, although I did know this was a conversation we'd need to have. All I can do is apologise. I should have had better control over my emotions.

"Accepting this is over..." He breathed in deeply. "I realise why you've made the decisions you have. You were made to feel unimportant, and that's something I can't undo. However, I can give you your freedom. If you want to divorce then I'm not going to fight it."

"Be honest with me. Do you want a divorce?"

"I don't know what I want. With Kingston now in my hands, I have some planning to do, so that's what I'm going to be focusing on for now. Give me a week, and then we can talk again, but the money I'll send to your account today. That's something I knew had to be separate from the contract."

"Yeah, it did." I bit down on my bottom lip. "Call me when you're ready for the conversation."

"Of course. Goodbye, Lou."

"No matter what happens between us, I do still care about you. Look after yourself, Cole."

He laughed, and then hung up on me. For a moment, I held the phone to my ear, before I pulled it away, looking at it. Did he believe I cared about him? He should have, but things were very different between us. At least he'd been honest with me about the PC, so I'd be able to get something new to start working on, even though it wasn't something I anticipated having to do.

With that conversation over, the next number I dialled was Katie's. "Contract signed?"

"Everything is sorted, but I'm not going to be able to start working straight away."

"Okay, what happened?"

"Unfortunately, Cole destroyed it. He is paying for a replacement, and I believe it was in a moment of madness, but it's definitely a new problem I didn't imagine I was going to have."

"Destroying a PC takes some work."

"I know, and it's a good reason for us to end our personal relationship too, because he needs to work through what that means. The person I fell in love with would never have done anything like that. He's no longer the same man, but I guess that's to be expected.

"Sometimes these things can be forgiven, especially as he was willing to make amends. He might have surprised himself, not knowing how strong the emotions were, considering what he's been like recently. You said it was like he'd turned them off, for reasons you didn't understand."

Nodding, I raked my hand through my hair. "Like I said, Cole's a very different person now. We used to be able to talk about anything, and he was comfortable with the fact that he had emotions. I feel like becoming Kingston Interactive had an effect on that, so now he feels like he shouldn't have emotions because he's a businessman." I shook my head. "I don't know. Getting into his head hasn't exactly been the easiest thing to do recently."

"Maybe this will change things, and you won't end up divorcing."

"For right now, I believe we will because I can't imagine staying married to him any longer. At the same time, things might be different next week. We're going to talk again when he's ready for the divorce conversation, even though I can't be certain it will actually happen. If it does, then we'll definitely end up divorcing."

CHAPTER-6

Fortunately, the money came through exactly as Cole said it would, giving me a chance to think through what I needed for my work PC, and I made the decision to go a company that made it for me. That might cost more, but I'd never built a PC before. Going through the different parts, working through each of the different options, I built something that was better than my old one, because I had the money to be able to do it.

Having something capable of doing everything I wanted it to was the most important thing. There were certain things I was thinking about doing, as the only developer of the newly created creative arm of Patterson's, to build up my following more than before, and then I'd hopefully bring in the kind of money there as I did at Kingston's. Maybe I'd even get more, as I was part of a known company, rather than going from nothing, the way I had with Cole.

With the PC about a week away from reaching me, I thought the time had come for us to make the announcement. I sent Katie a quick message, to tell her I was as ready as I was ever going to be, I watched social media, waiting for the moment it came up. I probably should have told Cole personally, but it was a conversation I didn't think would do either of us any good.

As it came up, and the responses started coming in, there was excitement from people who knew something about me. Moving over to my own personal accounts I wrote my own quick message about working with Katie, and getting more responses. Something I'd always tried to do was respond to some of those messages, so that's what I focused on for the afternoon because it was an easy thing to do with the laptop.

My phone made a sound beside me, and I glanced at it to see a text from Cole. All it said was one word - congratulations. He knew. He wasn't reacting badly, at least outwardly, but it might be harder for him internally because he knew there was a time when Patterson's wanted to work with us. Turning them down was a choice he'd made for Kingston. I hadn't agreed with it, and he knew it, so maybe it wasn't a surprise that I'd chosen to work with her.

The only option I had was to keep moving forward. We had a planned schedule for releases, giving me a couple of weeks to get settled before I started working on new IPs I'd been putting off. I had so many things I wanted to do, and now I finally felt like I could do what I'd been thinking of for months.

Going back to my social media, and reading through the responses, I could see how happy people were that I'd be somewhere I was able to do more. Katie, it seemed, had already shared some of the plans we had for future development. The games we wanted to bring out were something they seemed to be fascinated by.

***

One of the worst parts of having to wait for the new PC was not having something I could work on as easily. There were things I could do on the laptop, but it was old because I hadn't thought about updating it before. It was simply there as a backup option I didn't think I was actually going to need. Obviously, that was something I'd need to think about when I had a chance.

It was enough to do some of the basic coding and work through some of the stories I had planned. Being free to work on the ones I'd first developed, seeing how I'd changed in the time I'd been creating games, and going over certain things I would have changed had I been more experienced, was one of the most enjoyable elements.

I'm noting down what those changes would be, to move into other games. As tempting as it was to go back, I knew better than to do something like that. The best thing to do was move forward, keeping myself from making the same mistakes in the future, although it was likely I'd make different mistakes in those games.

Katie, every so often, sent an email, asking me what I was working on. She was actually interested, unlike Cole. Whenever I tried to talk to him about the games I was working on, he had basically shut me down. It was purely me who thought about what we needed if we were going to be able to make Kingston Interactive a success. Sighing, I bit down on my bottom lip, telling myself to stop.

"Be patient with yourself." The words Katie had said before came back to me. "Kingston was an important part of your life for a long time. Making the decision to move on, to leave it behind, is one thing. Actually, being able to do it is another entirely. You believed it was going to be your future, the same way you believed Cole would be. Now things are different, and it's going to take time for you to let go of it, however much you might want it to be done with right now."

Patience wasn't easy. Breathing in deeply, emotions swirling, I found myself looking at my phone, thinking about calling Cole. We'd said a week, and I knew I should leave it until he was ready. The conversation would have been much easier then, but I missed him. Closing my eyes, seeing him the way I had when we were first together, I picked up the phone and started scrolling through the gallery.

During the time we'd been working on Kingston we hadn't taken a lot of photos together, and it was strange to see the ones from before. The man I fell in love with was gone. The emotions in his eyes, the softness of his touch, the way he'd listen to me talk about anything… a tear trickled down my cheek, but I wiped it away, not wanting to cry over him again.

Then my phone rang. Seeing Cole's name sent a shiver of emotion through me, a mix of so many of them that I had no idea which was which, and I answered it. "Hi, Cole."

"As I've been thinking about the future, I thought it was best for me to call you." There was no emotion in his voice, the same way it had been for far too long. "I've made the decision; I believe it would be best for us to go through a divorce, because this obviously isn't a relationship either of us wants to be in now, so I've started talking to a lawyer to get it all sorted."

I stared at the wall, wondering if he had any regrets, I blinked, before slowly nodding. "Okay. If that's what you think is best, then I'm not going to argue against it."

"With Kingston needing my undivided attention moving forward I don't believe I can be the partner you need me to be. I'm sorry."

He didn't sound sorry. "So am I. I wish we could have spent the rest of our lives together, the way we planned."

"Lives change. We both knew that, and there was always a chance that everything would change until we got to the point where our lives no longer worked together."

"Yeah, I know." I breathed in deeply. "I still miss you."

For the first time, I sat in Katie's office. I went through the contract again, double-checking it even though we'd agreed on it weeks before, making certain everything was the way we said it would be. When I looked at her, she smiled. Had she been in my position I was certain she'd do the same thing.

"This protects your IP when you're going through a divorce, because until we declare our working relationship is over, that's going to be under the Iron Phoenix name."

Iron Phoenix was the name we'd finally come up with, both of us liking it more than any of the others, and I nodded. "Do you think Cole will go after it?"

"Anything is possible. That IP should be covered by the contract you signed with him when you split from Kingston Interactive, but people can make bad choices at times. With what he did to your PC it's definitely something we need to keep in mind, even though I doubt the man he was would have done any of this, and I feel like this is something he's going to be unhappy about."

"Possibly." I shrugged. "Whatever will be will be. He made his decision, and now I get to make mine." My eyes met with Katie's, as I signed the contracts, both our lawyers there to witness it. "Thank you."

"You have nothing to thank me for." She took her copy of it, putting it into her filing cabinet, and then the other two were given to our lawyers, so there were copies in multiple places. "Working together is something I've been hoping for ever since I first heard about you, and now it can finally happen."

Nodding, I smiled back, even though it faded quickly, my emotions were still a little more scattered than I needed them to be. Cole made the decision that it was best to get divorced was something I thought would happen, but I hoped we'd come to a different conclusion. Our lives together seemed better than they were when we were apart... until Kingston Interactive became a part of our lives.

"How about I introduce you to some of the people who work for the company so you can start to find your feet? I know you're going to be mostly working alone until we find some people to join you at Iron Phoenix, and you probably won't spend much time here. It's just something I think would be good for you as you move forward to get to know some of your colleagues, in case you need anything."

Getting to know them was a good way to keep my mind off everything. Nodding, I put my copy of the contract in my bag, picking it up as Katie stood. "How many people do you have working for you?"

"More than I think you're imagining at this point, Lou." She gestured for me to follow her. "I've been working in tech for a long time, and I like to gather the best of the best. Hence, me trying to get Kingston to work with us. Cole was good, but you were better."

Blinking, I stared at her. "I was better?"

Katie grinned. "Do you think I didn't read your bio on the Kingston site? I know what you did to become the developer you are now. You chose an interesting path to walk, considering the options you had because you didn't have to help Cole build Kingston Interactive into what it was."

"We'd been together for a long time. It didn't make sense not to try to do something." I shrugged. "When I first started, I had no idea if I was going to be able to help him. Cole got the Virtual School idea into his head, and he started working on the headsets because he thought that was the best place for us to start. When I started working on the games, he saw it as a distraction.

"Explaining to him why I'd made the decision I had was far harder than I wanted it to be. He didn't see how important it was for us to earn an income straight off, otherwise, we weren't going to get anywhere. He was okay with me working on my own projects eventually, although it was something he only wanted me to do when I wasn't coding for the school, and when I started to invest more of my income into the company, he accepted it without ever thanking me."

CHAPTER-7

The divorce was far simpler than I imagined it could be. Kingston Interactive was already dealt with, and Cole didn't show any interest in trying to take the IP from me. He truly didn't care. He'd already paid me for the computer, so we didn't have that to deal with either, but there were still some things I wanted from the house.

Cole was willing to let me go over at a point when he was at another talk, so we didn't have to spend any time together. Being in the house alone was strange, and when I left, after an hour to make sure I had everything together, I put my keys on the counter, knowing I'd never go back again.

Sighing, I looked at it one last time, before I got into my packed car. I thought I'd be done with all the emotions, but I wasn't. Cole had been a part of my life for so long that I knew it was going to take time to work through everything. I'd read somewhere it takes half the time you were in a relationship with someone for the grief to fade. Not that it seemed like he felt the same way.

Driving away, to my new apartment, I didn't feel like the weight was off my shoulders, even though it was. There was no going back. No more dealing with Kingston Interactive. I breathed in deeply, holding back the tears that were threatening to escape again. One day I'd stop crying. Unfortunately, it seemed like it was going to be far in the future.

I parked in my spot, planning on leaving unpacking for a little while, I stared into the distance, thinking about what might have been. How different our lives would have been had Cole and I been able to work through things, especially as I'd still be working on the games with Kingston Interactive. Our company. We'd built it up together from nothing, and, yes, it had led me to Iron Phoenix, but was that really what I wanted?

It wasn't as though I had any other option. Slipping out of the car, and grabbing a couple of bags to be useful, I made my way to the apartment, pulling the keys out of my pocket. I took a deep breath and stepped into the hallway. It was a nice place, although a lot smaller than the old house. Anything bigger would have been pointless as it was only me.

The bags needed to go into the bedroom, so I could start unpacking. I barely had anything compared to what I'd made the decision to leave behind because Cole would need it, and it was furniture we'd bought during our relationship. Fortunately, he'd been willing to give me a little extra financially to cover that loss.

Getting the furniture in place was something I'd done before I made the decision, I was going to move in. Paying extra for a short time didn't bother me too much, because I was getting more than enough from Iron Phoenix to cover it. Even though all we'd done so far was release the old Kingston Interactive games there was enough interest in my switch from one company to the other so they were making a nice amount of income.

We had two new games planned for release in the next month. One of them was a continuation of an older series, while the other was something entirely new. I didn't need to work as much as I had before, and I knew it, but working kept me from thinking too much about things I couldn't change.

My new office was comfortable. Even while I was still staying with Sarah and Alex, partly so I wouldn't spend all my nights thinking about my ex-husband, I came here to work, so at least some of the money I was paying was worth it. There was this voice in the back of my head telling me I'd be better off if I'd stayed there. That way I wouldn't think about Cole all the time. I knew better than to think I could spend the rest of my life living with my friends.

Alex and Sarah had their own lives to live. They could do that better without me. I also had a life to live, and I could do whatever I wanted with that life, however much I might have loved Cole. Sighing, I stepped into the office, knowing the best thing I could do was spend a couple of hours working.

***

Until my life changed, I hadn't thought about streaming. As I was spending the majority of my life entirely alone it had become strangely tempting, because it meant I could socialise without having to go anywhere. Katie thought it would help to increase interest in Iron Phoenix, so she backed me, although I knew she was more than willing to take me out if that was what I wanted.

Dealing with other people in real life wasn't something I was ready for. It wasn't as though I wouldn't get the same questions in chat, but then it was different. There was some distance between me and them. Random crying was slightly less embarrassing, especially as I could disconnect if I really needed to, and it wasn't as though they didn't already have an idea of what had happened. They knew something had led to me leaving Kingston Interactive to work at Patterson's, as the head of Iron Phoenix, and CCO.

Setting up my PC, I bit down on my bottom lip. There was also a chance no one would care. I was going to stream one of the games I'd developed, playing through the levels and talking about them, which I hoped would be interesting enough to draw in the viewers. Like others, I gave it ten minutes for viewers to gather.

Had no one appeared I could easily have disappeared, pretending it had never happened. Instead, I found myself with over 100 viewers before the end of the ten minutes, something I couldn't have imagined, and I put my headset on, telling myself everything was going to be fine.

"Good afternoon, everyone. Thank you for joining me as I experiment with streaming." I looked at the camera, trying to stay as normal as possible. "This is my first attempt at this, so please be gentle with me, while also letting me know if there are any issues with my equipment. Can everyone hear me okay?"

Receiving actual responses was like nothing I could have imagined. Fortunately, it seemed like the headset was fine, so I didn't need to change anything, and then I nodded. "Great. If anything changes give me a poke, because I know the balance might change when I actually get to the game. What I wanted to do first was have a little chat with you guys, and see how things are going now that I'm with Iron Phoenix.

"As I know, there are going to be questions about my decision to leave Kingston Interactive so I thought I'd start there." While I said the words, I saw exactly that. "I don't know exactly what everyone knows, so I'll start at the beginning, for those of you who are new. Up until a couple of days ago, I was Louise Kingston." I sighed. "Kingston Interactive is a company I built with my ex-husband, Cole.

"In the beginning, we worked well together." Lying probably wasn't the best option, but I didn't want people turning on Cole. "Then the time came when we were both focusing more on our own things than we were on our relationship because we basically worked on two different sides of the company.

"Cole was the one focused on the headsets and the Virtual School. That's still what he's doing now, continuing with Kingston Interactive, so please support him with that if you can. Honestly, the school is amazing. Even if you aren't taking lessons, some of the experiences, we built together are worth going on as adults, especially as we did a lot of work to make it as realistic as possible, and I have a lot of love for it.

"Even though I was a part of the work being done for the school, I was doing the majority of the work on the games." All the work, because Cole never had any interest in the games, which was something they also didn't need to know. "Due to this, we had far less time to spend together as people. We were like ships in the night at times.

"Sometimes, as much as you love someone, the time comes when you aren't compatible any longer. We made that decision, and he was willing to let me take my intellectual property, knowing how much time I'd put into it, so I could continue working on a series he knew you loved. He never wanted to take that away from you, which means we will be moving forward with some series you might have thought were over."

My phone rang, and I reached out to pick it up without looking at it. "Hello?"

"Lou."

"Cole?" I raked my hand through my hair. "What are you calling for?"

There was a moment of silence, and he breathed in deeply. "I saw your stream."

Blinking, I stared at the screen in front of me. "You had time for that?"

"Well, not exactly, but I got a call from a couple of investors, who wanted me to watch it, especially the early parts." I could almost see him biting his lip as he tried to find the words. "Thank you."

"Do you have something to thank me for?"

"At no point in the entire stream did you throw me under the bus, even though you could have done so. You spoke about Kingston Interactive with love, and I appreciate that more than you can know because you didn't have to do that. After everything I did..." He sighed. "I watched some of the talks I gave, and there was never a point when I mentioned you, or the work you did, or the effort you put into keeping our business running.

"You deserved better than that. I heard the way you talked about everything… you spent two hours playing a game, answering questions kindly, and I realised I made a mistake. I know it's done. There's no going back, and I'm as okay with that as I can be, but I wanted you to know I'm sorry.

"I should have said it before. I should have told you how much you meant to me. You still do, even now that we're divorced, but it was the right thing to do. I'm not a good partner right now. Maybe, in time, I will be, when things are different. For now, though, I do need to focus on Kingston, because you were the main income."

My first response was one I kept myself from saying because he'd just thanked me for being kind. I wasn't going to undo that. "Let me know if there's anything I can do."

"Focus on yourself, Louise. Even when I was being a fool you still tried to give me chances, ones I didn't realise I needed, and you shouldn't be giving me another one now."

Laughing, I shook my head. "I wouldn't be me, Cole, if I didn't."

He laughed too, joining me. "Okay, you're right about that. I might call again in the future. Maybe we can start as friends again."

"Maybe we can. I need to get back to work, but good luck with everything you're doing with Kingston."

"Good luck with Iron Phoenix."

Seconds later, he was gone, and I put the phone down on the desk. Of course, it was after we'd got divorced that Cole realised the mistakes he'd made. There was no going back. Even if we did manage to become friends again, I wasn't sure I could imagine us ever being in a romantic relationship in the future.

CHAPTER-8

atie sat opposite me, the planned schedule on the screen beside her, and she didn't look happy. "Lou…"

"Am I not working hard enough?"

She blinked, shaking her head. "No, it's not that, at all." She put her hand over mine. "Be honest with me. Is this how much you were working before when you were living with Cole."

Nodding, I raked my free hand through my hair. "I like working, Katie. This…" I looked at the screen. "You're worried about me."

"Of course, I'm worried about you. I appreciate everything you're doing for Iron Phoenix, and I know why you're doing as much as you are. What you are working on is amazing, but you're going to burn out, which is not what we need. I want you to start planning for some time off."

"Time off is hard." I breathed in deeply. "Even now I find myself thinking too much, and that... well, I've been trying to avoid it as much as possible. The divorce was the right thing, but doing the right thing often isn't easy."

"I can help with that. There's a convention I was planning on sending Iron Phoenix to if you're willing to make the journey, and I thought I could join you, to help you keep your mind off Cole."

"Conventions aren't something I've ever thought about before, even though I probably should have done."

"Well, I can show you what I was thinking." She turned the screen, so I could see it a little better. "It's relatively local, but I would still suggest getting a room nearby, in case we end up drinking." She glanced at me. "There are a couple of things we could get involved with, and then, if this goes well, we can start going to more, to build up interest in Iron Phoenix."

"Honestly, Katie, if you think it's a good idea, then I'm willing to try."

Sighing, her eyes met mine. "Louise..."

"Yes, I know, I'm not sounding enthusiastic. I think it's a good idea, but it's not something I think would have crossed my mind at any point. Something we probably need to think about is merchandise, for some of the series we're working on, I can work on that in the next couple of weeks. It's also something we could probably use to sell generally."

"Why is it that when I try to get you to take time off, I end up making you plan on taking up more work." Katie laughed. "As long as you promise me, you're going to take at least a night off when we're at the convention."

"I promise." It was a promise I might not be able to keep, but I'd do my best. "This could be fun, though, because I've never had a chance to do merchandise before, and experimenting with something new is always fun."

Grinning, Katie nodded. "As long as you keep me up to date, so we don't have to carry too much."

***

Turning to social media, to find out what people would buy in the way of Iron Phoenix merchandise, I set up a poll before starting work on some ideas. I wasn't willing to wait for answers when I could start work. Some options were worth testing out even if the poll said otherwise, because I could always sell them elsewhere.

I started focusing on designs that might be used on multiple items I started sketching. Cole didn't know how much work went into the games when I started working on them, to begin with, because we hadn't had the money to hire other people to work on them, so I'd done a lot of the early artwork. Going back to that was well worth it, as I started planning out what we might be able to do.

Someone else had designed the logo for Iron Phoenix, and I knew Katie was getting in contact with them to see if we could extend the contract to merchandise. I'd done the same with some of my artists, asking them if they wanted to be a part of it, and if they did, I already had some contracts set up.

One of the things I'd found early on was that respect got me respect. Showing the artists that I understood how much time went into their work, both as they were doing it and the years it took to get to that point, got me respect in return. Having artists who liked me got me some extras I'd never expected, the most interesting one being recommended as an employer, so if I needed a new artist, then there were those who already knew about me.

As I finished up a potential design, based on one of the scenes from the very first games I coded, I received my first response. The artist in question was one I'd worked with on a series of games, and she already had a few ideas for what we could do for merchandise. Smiling, I asked if she wanted to chat.

When she said yes, I got things set up and then called her. "This is going to be so much fun, Lou." She grinned. "I was hoping the time would come when you'd start doing conventions for the games. At one of the recent ones, I went to, I saw someone dressed as one of the characters from the game."

"You did?" I bit down on my bottom lip. "I didn't think that had happened yet."

"Creating characters people love is a skill of yours, which is why I agreed to be one of your artists. Until you sent me an email, I hadn't thought about working in games. So many people have horror stories to tell about their experience but you were kind, considerate, and respectful. It helped me to make the decision because I didn't think I'd end up with one of those stories. Instead, I was able to share your name with other artists who might want work."

"I always did my best to be someone I'd want to work with, so I did at least achieve that."

"Better than almost anyone I've worked with." Beth studied me. "There are a couple of artists I can suggest who might be able to take on the task of working with me to build up a merchandise line for the series, if that's what you want to do."

"For now, we're doing a small amount of merchandise to see how well they're going to sell, before we make any decision as to what the next steps are going to be. You think we'll be able to get somewhere?"

"Due to the size of your following, I have no reason to think you won't. I know you aren't paying a lot of attention to that. Your focus is on the games right now, especially as you're starting afresh with Iron Phoenix, but the reason people love the games you make is you. They'd have gone anywhere, as long as they were able to get something you created.

"More than anything, I feel you need to understand why people love your games. You create amazing characters who live through interesting experiences, and that's what they want. The worlds you've built are so interesting, a sign of the work you've been putting in to make everything come together. People want to play your games to explore those worlds, which is why they buy more, so you can make more."

***

At the end of the day, my poll told me very little because things were very even. Smiling, I went through the list of artists, and what they were going to be doing. The things they suggested most were pins, because they thought an Iron Phoenix pin collection would sell well.

With the pins, we were also going to have a selection of fabric items, although I wasn't sure which would sell best. This was all going to be an experiment, the same way the games were, and I sent the email I'd been working on off to Katie. It was then I looked at the time, to find it was far later than I'd thought.

Before I got complained at, I shut down the computer. Even though my mind was too full of ideas, so full I didn't think I'd be able to sleep, I got ready for bed, trying to prepare myself to get some sleep. Just being in pyjamas didn't help my brain to slow down in any way, especially as I was working on something entirely new.

I lay down, staring up at the ceiling, seeing images in front of my eyes. Some were images I'd drawn, sketches for worlds I knew as well as I knew my own apartment. Others were drawn by my group of artists, the call I had with Beth slowly grew until there were eight of us working on different ideas, planning out different options incase things went well.

Eventually, we had a full series of pins for each of the worlds I'd created. They were going to be released at different times, and we were talking about potential exclusives, which would likely be the same pins that had some extra sparkle. Some would be glittery, and others would be more metallic, only available for sale at different conventions, but if we did that, I would make certain that people could get them if they wanted them.

I closed my eyes, I breathed in deeply, trying to stop my thoughts. It wasn't the easiest of things for me to do. Once, there would have been someone I could talk to in the middle of the night about things I was planning, although it hadn't happened for a long time. Rolling onto my side, teeth buried in my bottom lip for a moment, I thought about how long it had been.

The games weren't something Cole was interested in, so any time I shared my plans with him he didn't much care about them. At the same time, he liked it when I listened to his plans for the headsets and the Virtual School, especially when I shared my ideas about that with him, until the time came when even that wasn't something we talked about much.

He was slowly fading me out. I thought about it, no longer affected in the same way by the emotion, trying to remember when we last talked about the school. There was a chance it might have been before the new year, back when things were still okay between us. After that everything changed.

Why had it changed? It wasn't something I ever asked him, because I wasn't sure I wanted the answer, even though I probably should have. Then we might have been able to keep working together. Of course, even if we had been able to work together that didn't mean our personal relationship would have gotten better. That was dead, however many times I tried to save it.

Unlike me, Cole cared more about Kingston Interactive. I cared more about our relationship, and yet I probably wouldn't have given up my IP in order for us to survive, so maybe I was wrong about that. Maybe I cared more about what I was capable of doing. Sighing, I rolled onto my back again. Of course, my thoughts had turned to Cole.

Moving on, even after a divorce, wasn't as easy as I hoped it would be. Every so often he'd be right there in my mind, and I couldn't get rid of him. It wasn't unexpected. I was barely a month out from the divorce. There was a part of me that still loved him. Would it always love him? Could I move on, and build a new relationship, with someone who'd appreciate me? Did I want to? That was the more complicated question. Was there a good reason for me to be in a relationship with someone else in the future?

CHAPTER-9

awing, I poured myself the third coffee of the morning, and Katie looked at me. "How much sleep did you get last night?"

"Barely any." I shrugged. "Unfortunately, insomnia's been hitting me hard recently. My mind doesn't really turn off at the moment."

"Do you want to talk about it?"

I shook my head. "Talking about it probably won't help all that much. Cole won't stop haunting me for a while yet." I sighed, sitting down opposite her. "Our relationship has only been over for a couple of months, and I know it's going to take time for me to work through the emotions. A part of me does still love him."

"Of course, it does." Blinking, I looked at Katie. "The two of you were together for a long time, Lou. I'd be more worried if you didn't feel the way you do, especially as I know it was a slow death, making it even harder."

"Surely a slow death would make it easier to move on."

"Not when you were the one trying to keep it alive. I remember the conversations we had before, and how much effort you put into fixing the problems you had. Only Cole wasn't willing to do anything himself. Seeing that… honestly, it was hard to understand, because I've never been married. I've never loved someone the way you obviously loved Cole. Work has always been my focus, so it was strange, but then I knew I would do whatever I had to in order to save the company if something went wrong."

"Cole didn't." I ran my tongue over my bottom lip. "That's something I've been thinking about a lot the last few days, while we've been working to build up the merchandise for Iron Phoenix." I breathed in deeply. "By the time we split, Cole had truly come to think of Kingston Interactive as his company, not ours. He didn't actually care if I left, whatever he might have said, because he'd slowly been icing me out for about six months.

"Even though I was bringing in the majority of the money with the games it was as though that wasn't happening." I shook my head. "It's hard to put into words, Katie, because I didn't even realise it was happening until I had a chance to look back. A couple of nights ago I was thinking about the last time I felt like I could have a conversation with someone about what I was working on.

"Things changed around the new year. I don't know what happened, but there was something off, and I couldn't quite put my finger on it. He stopped talking to me about the school, and the headset. That was something we used to do together, but he was never interested in the games. Like I said before, he thought of them as a distraction, rather than a way of making money, however much they brought in. What I did never quite seemed to be enough for him."

"Working with the people we care about is never easy." Katie sipped her own coffee. "Before I started this company, because I needed to get away from my family, I worked with my dad. We have a much better relationship now, partly due to us not spending so much time together. At the time, though, I think it had actually gotten to the point where we might have hated each other, and there were a number of reasons for that.

"Dad was the boss. He was someone who didn't like to be questioned, or told there might be another way of doing things. Sometimes I'd try to bring up an idea I had only to have it shot down, as he had no interest in change, especially not if I was the one who suggested it. To him I was still a child. Why would my ideas be of any use?

"Planning out how to get away was something I started doing about six months before I left because I knew I couldn't stay there any longer. Even though my dad wasn't happy with me for leaving, even though he didn't have a reason for me to stay, and it took me another year to start actually making some income from Patterson's.

"For a long time, it wasn't something I could talk to Dad about. He didn't want to know what I was doing. Then, slowly, he started thawing, as he put the pieces together. Someone else was complaining about how he was treating his employees, and he realised the damage he'd done to our relationship."

"After I did the first stream, Cole called me. He said his investors told him about what I was doing. I think they might have been worried I was going to say something against Kingston Interactive."

"Instead of that, you did the opposite." Katie smiled. "You got a lot of supporters from that, by choosing to be kind to your ex."

"Being kind is a part of who I am. Had I done something different it would have been very strange." I shrugged. "It seems to be something Cole forgot about me too, but he did apologise to me for the way he'd treated me before. Of course, it means less now that I have realised, he was trying to get rid of me, and in the end, all I did was what he wanted me to."

"Unless he's realised it's not what I wanted, Lou. You know it's possible, especially as you took the majority of the money away, and now he has to live with that."

Slowly, I nodded, wondering if that was why he'd called. Did he think I was going to offer to go back to Kingston Interactive? I sighed. He did tell me to stop being so nice, maybe because he knew what he'd done before, and that was just when I offered to help him with Kingston. The likelihood was he didn't want me back, but that didn't mean he didn't want the money I could bring in.

We continued working through the list of options, when one of the guys came in with a box. Katie smiled, standing to take it from him, and he smiled back. "Thank you, Mark." She turned to me. "These are the pens."

"The pens?"

"Yes, the pens." She put the box down on her desk, and opened it. "The Iron Phoenix pens. Our logo maker helped me adapt it for them."

I raised an eyebrow, taking the pen she held out to me, I looked at it. It was a plain black ballpoint pen, with Iron Phoenix on it. "What are they for?"

"Giving away. Pens are one of our best ways of sharing the name. I thought about getting business cards, but these are more useful."

Nodding, I slowly turned the pen, seeing the name of the website on the other side of it. "Okay, that kind of makes sense." I tried it on one of the pieces of paper near me. "The pen isn't bad either."

"A good pen, with our name on it, is exactly what I was hoping for. I want you to take that with you when we're at the convention. There should also be some pins for you to wear, so people can see them, because there are a number of them in production now."

"How much of this is for Patterson's?"

"Barely any." Katie's eyes met with mine. "You know as well as I do that a lot of the tech work is done in the background, but you're something entirely different. Having a game development division was something I'd been wanting to do for a long time, Lou, and having you join me is exactly what I needed, because Iron Phoenix is perfect. People already know you, so they are going to follow you anywhere.

"With so much going on in the background we have a lot of money to put into Iron Phoenix, and that's what I'm going to keep doing. This is how we build up to have multiple game developers working with us, whole teams planning on new worlds, and it won't all be on your shoulders."

Katie, of course, thought taking it off my shoulders was going to be a good thing. I gave her a smile, trying to act as normal as possible, even though there was uncertainty building within me. What we were doing was exciting. I was enjoying preparing for the convention, and it was something I was looking forward to. At the same time, I couldn't imagine sharing my job with someone else, however logical it might be, after all the time I'd spent doing it alone.

Saying that to Katie wasn't something I was ready to do. "Let's see how things go at the convention first." I looked at my pen. "There's no way of knowing what might happen when we're there."

"Even if it doesn't go amazingly well, I'm certain we'll make all the money we spent on it back."

Sarah's eyes met with mine. "Lou..."

"I know. I should be happy Katie has plans for Iron Phoenix. She's obviously excited about it. I just... giving up control isn't something I'm entirely comfortable with."

Nodding, Sarah put her hand on mine. "I understand. When you were at Kingston, with it being a company you built up with Cole, you were completely in control, and you were always going to be. Now you're not, because Katie's involved, and that... well, it's going to take time to get used to."

Looking down into my coffee, I sighed. "I don't know that I want to get used to it."

"You want to leave Iron Phoenix?"

"Maybe. Everything is very complicated right now, Sarah. Before things fell apart with Cole, I had all kinds of plans for the game division. After what happened with Katie there was a disconnect, and I took a slight step back from some of those plans, because I didn't know whether it was the right thing to do.

"Although I know Katie's excited, and she thinks this is amazing, I'm getting to the point where I feel the same way. The last thing I want is to walk away from this without thinking it through, but maybe I'm not meant to be working with someone else. Maybe I'm meant to be doing this alone, rather than be a part of something."

"For now, I think you need to do the convention, because you've both put a lot of work into this, and possibly talk to Katie about how you feel."

"Talking to her probably would be a good idea." I breathed in deeply, drinking my coffee rather than staring at it. "She honestly thought it was what I wanted. How could she not? Sharing how I'm feeling with her will help, if she's willing to listen to me, but sometimes I go back to how things were with Cole. He wasn't someone who was good at listening to me."

"Remember, Katie isn't Cole. Share how you're feeling with her, and what you want to do with Iron Phoenix. Don't hold back your feelings purely because you're scared. She isn't Cole."

"No, she's not." I smiled. "You're right. I need to be honest with her, and honest with myself. First, though, I need to work out what it is I want from all of this. Do I want to work alone? Do I want to work with other people?" I shrugged. "Katie and I talked a lot about the future before, but there was no way I could know this was going to happen until it did."

"Of course not. You've never worked this way with anyone other than Cole."

"That's more than enough about me. Sometimes I feel like all we ever talk about is my problems. I want you to talk to me about your life."

Laughing, Sarah shook her head. "You know I don't mind helping you through things like this. You're my best friend, Lou. I know if the same thing happened to me then you'd be there for me in the same way."

CHAPTER-10

"Lou, your IP is your IP." Katie looked at me, her eyes meeting with mine, and I could see the understanding in them. "When I was talking about building up Iron Phoenix it was with other developers doing their own thing." She smiled. "No one, unless you want them to, will be working on any of your games.

"My excitement is because I'm starting something I've been planning for a long time. Now that I'm working with you it means I might be able to convince other developers to join us, doing their own thing, with the main branch possibly getting a different name, if that's what you'd prefer. For now, it's simply the division name, but I know you're Iron Phoenix."

Nodding, I bit down on my bottom lip. "I need to think about what I want, Katie, because, as much as this seemed like it was exactly what I wanted, I'm not sure now." I raked a hand through my hair. "This… it's complicated. I know a lot of my emotions are still all over the place, and

I don't want to make a decision about any of this until I've worked through some of them."

"Of course. When we wrote the contract, we said there was a six-month period where either one of us could pull out without there being any issues." Katie put her hand over mine. "You can talk to me about this as much or as little as you want. I know how complicated things are right now."

"I am sorry. I know how much you've done to make this possible. The plan is to stay with you until the convention, because we've both put a lot of time into it, and after that, I'll work through what it is I want to do next. I don't want either of us to be in limbo."

"Don't apologise, Lou. You're being honest with me, and that's all I asked of you. I said before how complicated my relationship with Dad was, the two of us working together because we didn't have any other option until the time came when I could leave. The last thing I want to do is trap someone in a position they don't want to be in. You need to tell me exactly what you need from me, to make this easier on you."

"All I need is time. The decision is one I can only make alone. I just…Thank you for understanding. I do appreciate it, because I don't know what I'd do if this had gone badly. I knew it was unlikely, but with how things went when I tried to talk to Cole…"

"Everything is okay between us. I'm not Cole, and this isn't Kingston. We'll find a way through this, one way or another, okay? Even if that means you leaving to do your own thing."

***

Reaching out with one hand, I answered the phone, not looking at who was calling again. "Hi, Lou."

"I swear we've talked more in the last three weeks than we did in the last three months of our marriage."

Cole laughed. "Do I apologise for that?"

"Maybe. I don't know. This is weird. Why do you keep calling me?"

"Sometimes I miss you."

"Why do you miss me?"

"Oh, there are so many reasons. I think I got to the point where I took you for granted, and I shouldn't have, because now you aren't here you seem to be the only thing I can think about."

"Aren't you also thinking about the school?"

"You know what I mean." There was a tinge of frustration in his voice. "If you don't want me to call all you have to do is ask, and I'll stop."

"Honestly, Cole, I don't know what it is I want. You did mention being friends, but this…" I shrugged. "I don't know if we can be friends, after being married. There's a part of me that does still love you, and I have no idea if this is something we should be doing, because it might mean I can never move on."

The silence went on for longer than I thought it would. "I don't know if I can move on." He breathed in deeply, and I could hear the emotions in his voice for the first time in far too long. "Like I said, you're the only thing I can think about. I close my eyes, and you're right there. I open them again, and all of this feels like a dream, so when I roll over, you're going to be there. Only, you aren't."

"No, I'm not, because you made the decision that it was best for the two of us to end our relationship. If you have regrets then that's on you. I was willing to see if we could make things work after we split Kingston in two."

"Lou, I was angry with you. You were walking away from Kingston, and it felt like you were walking away from me at the same time, so there was no reason for us to keep trying. Only when the anger faded did I start to regret the choice I'd made. You've made it pretty obvious you don't feel like there's any way back now."

"Right now, I don't know." I wished he was in front of me, so he could see me, rather than us having the conversation over the phone. "I loved you, Cole, and I know you were trying to freeze me out of Kingston for a while, without ever talking to me about the problem you had."

"Finding the right words was hard. I wanted to talk to you, but I didn't know how, and I know that's not a good reason for what I did. Hurting you is something I should never have done. You were my wife first, and my business partner second, until the time came when you felt like you weren't either of those things.

"Your decision to focus on the gaming side of things felt wrong, when I was putting so much of my time into the school. Before you say anything, I know you were also putting your time into the school, but it didn't feel like it was enough, especially as it wasn't making anywhere near as much money as I hoped it would. From the beginning you were making me.

"It made me feel like my business idea meant nothing. The school... I don't know how to put this into words, Lou, even after everything we've been through. You were so much better at things than I was. I was barely capable of creating the headsets, and there you were, taking on multiple jobs, including being the main income for Kingston."

"Basically, you were jealous."

"Putting it all into one word." Cole sighed. "Yes, I was jealous, and I didn't know how to tell you, because at first, I wanted you to be successful, in part due to it meaning that Kingston was successful. Unfortunately, it wasn't enough. I wanted Kingston to be successful because of me, and I still do. I just don't know if it's going to be possible."

"Maybe it's not. I don't know. All I know is that if you've made your choices, you have to live with them. I'm not going to join Kingston again."

***

"We have a new shipment in." Katie drew me into her office. "It's the first of the pins."

Nodding, I went with her, trying to find my excitement, when all I could think about was the conversation I'd had with Cole. I felt like I'd been unkind to him. He was being honest with me, and I should have been grateful for that.

Sighing, I glanced at Katie, wondering if it was something I should talk about with her.

"Maybe today isn't the best time for this." She looked at me. What happened, Lou?"

"Cole called last night." I bit down on my bottom lip as I looked at the pins scattered on the desk. "They are beautiful." I picked one of them up, looking at the design, and smiled. "This was a good idea."

"Of course, it was. Pins are something people really love, because they're easy to collect, and we can make them for different series, to make it worthwhile to start building up those collections." She ran her finger over one of them. "Do you want to talk about Cole?"

"Yes, and no." I breathed in deeply. "He was talking to me about Kingston, and how he was jealous of me. I was more capable than he was at doing a number of different things, especially making money for the company, something he wanted to be able to do alone."

"He can do that now."

"I said something similar." I shrugged. "If he has regrets, he has to live with them because I'm not going backwards. However much I might not be certain of the choices I've made since then; I still refuse to return to Kingston."

"Good. You deserve better than that." She put her hand on my shoulder. "I do understand how he feels because I've been there at times. When I see what you're capable of, I'm sometimes jealous. You're amazing, in so many different ways, and I wish I could channel your skills at time, but that's not a good reason to treat someone badly. Especially if that's someone you say you love."

"Amazing?"

"Yes, Lou, amazing." She grinned, and her eyes met mine. "I get the feeling you haven't been told that enough. Not by Cole, or anyone else."

"There are people who have called me amazing in the past, but it's not something I ever truly accepted. Everything I've done to get to where I am was more luck than anything. If it hadn't been for Cole, I never would have started coding, and I know I have a lot to thank him for, even if there are a lot of reasons for me to be upset with him. This is a life I never would have led without him.

"Sometimes I can't help thinking I wanted him here, to see what we've done. He was so against what I was doing at the time. Now... well, it's not as though I haven't talked about this before. Emotions are complicated, and they're something I'm still working through. That's going to be harder than I wanted it to be, I think because I do still love him. Talking to him last night simply reminded me of that."

"Love isn't enough. Not when the two of you didn't have a good relationship outside of that because he couldn't communicate with you."

"Had he been able to, we might have been able to work through his jealousy together, but he wasn't willing to talk to me."

"Admitting to those kinds of complicated emotions isn't the easiest thing to do. I can understand him not being ready, and I still think it's something he had to do, if he wanted the two of you to stay together."

"Yeah, he did." I looked at her. "You said you were never in love."

"Business and love are very similar things. One of the most important things in business is also the ability to communicate with your employees. I've found that everything is easier on all of us if I work through what I wanted to say in advance, share my thoughts, and then listen to what everyone else has to say. If I shut them out, we wouldn't be where we are now."

"Cole shut me out, leading to a divorce. He said, once, he loved me, and I believed that until the time came to prove it."

"That's why I said before, if you have any issues, I want you to talk to me about them. Working through what you're feeling is something we can do together, so you can make the best possible decision. Even if you make the decision to leave, I'll support you, Lou, because you're a friend now."

CHAPTER-11

Getting set up for the convention was easier than I thought it was going to be. Katie liked being prepared, and she'd done a lot of work to make the job as easy as possible, so unpacking at our stall, already surrounded by people, took less time than I expected. A couple of people were already exploring our new Iron Phoenix pin collections.

"These are beautiful." One of the younger women looked at the pins, running her fingers over them. "How much are they?"

"$10 a pin, but we do offer deals for more than one." I thought it was too much, which was a sign I knew very little about merchandise because Katie told me that was the best price for us to go with. "I believe it was $2 off each extra pin, and if you buy the full collection for any series, you basically get one pin free."

Nodding, she smiled. "I need to make a decision about which one I want to get."

"Do you have a favourite character?"

"Working that out is what makes it so complicated." Her eyes met mine for a moment. "There are so many of the characters I'd call a favourite I don't know where to start." She looked back at the pins. "I'll be back."

As she walked away, I watched her go. Should I have pushed her to buy something? I bit down on my bottom lip, looking at Katie, who was talking to someone else. No, I shouldn't push anyone to buy anything. Being friendly was better than doing anything else because it would make people come back, and I turned back to start getting out some more of the pins.

Katie had pinboards prepared for each series, so I put them around the place, looking at some of the ones I hadn't yet seen. They were beautiful, and I grabbed one of my favourites, putting it on my jacket, before turning back to the growing crowd. I breathed in deeply, telling myself everything was going to be okay, I stepped forward a little.

"Can I help anyone?"

One of the younger guys at the front of the crowd looked at the pin on my jacket. "Is that your favourite character?"

"Honestly, I can't really call one of them a favourite. The others might get jealous."

My words made him look more closely at me. "Louise?"

"That's me."

"Oh, wow." He pulled something out of his bag. "I know this is super weird, but would you mind signing this for me?"

"No, of course not."

Taking the item, I looked at it. "Did you do this?"

"Yeah, I did. Your games have made me fascinated by the whole thing. I started with the art first, and now I'm starting to learn coding."

Pulling my Iron Phoenix pen out of my pocket I signed the picture, and then grabbed another to pass to him. "Send me an email if you want any help."

He stared at me for a moment. "You'd help me?"

"Everyone needs someone to give them a chance." I smiled. "You need anything, let me know."

"Thank you."

As he left, I felt other people looking at me, and I turned to them, doing my best to keep a smile on my lips. "Does anyone else need my help?"

"Will you be signing some of the other pictures?"

Blinking, I looked down at them. "A lot of the artwork isn't by me."

"No, but you created the characters, and they do already have the artist's signature on them. Having both would make them worth more."

"Okay, let me know which ones you want. I'll sign whichever ones you choose to buy."

Somehow, I'd become a person people wanted to autograph things. I wasn't quite certain how it happened, but it had, and it was something I was going to have to learn to live with. As two of the customers picked out their pictures, choosing a couple of the most expensive ones, I signed my name on them, making certain I didn't put it over the artist's signature.

I took the money, unable to believe how much people were paying for it, I glanced at Katie. "You're doing really well. People like you, Lou, and that's the most important thing."

***

My hand was sore. I didn't know how many pictures I'd signed, but it was far more than I had planned, and I hadn't known I was going to need to sign any of them. Katie flopped down beside me, looking as exhausted as I felt. She put her head on my shoulder, looking like she might be able to fall asleep, even though we definitely had a bed we could go to.

"Come on, Kate. We need to get something to eat, and then we need to get some sleep before tomorrow morning."

"Tomorrow?" She looked at me. "Whose stupid idea was this?"

"Don't go there." Standing, I hauled her up, and she sighed shaking her head. "Come on. There has to be somewhere we can get something quickly."

"I planned it out. We have a place just up the road where we should be able to get something to eat." She breathed in deeply. "Okay, I can do this." Katie smiled, although it still looked like all she wanted to do was go to bed, which was honestly what I felt too. "Come on. I'll lead the way."

Other people were also leaving the convention, in a way that made me think they were also sellers. Everyone was packed up, ready to go out again tomorrow, and then on Monday. I glanced at Kate. She looked back at me, her eyes meeting mine. There was an apology within them, because she had no idea how busy things would be.

"When I suggested it, I thought we might get a small crowd, people who were interested in what you were doing, but it turned out there were far more people than I imagined who wanted to have some Iron Phoenix merchandise. You being willing to sign things increased the interest."

"A willingness I now regret." I looked at my hand. "Especially as I'm not going to be able to say no now. I've already started signing things, so I'm going to have to keep doing it. Next time, if there is a next time, I'll do that over the weeks before the convention, rather than doing them all on the three convention days."

"Honestly, I think it would be for the best, and I have no reason to think there won't be a next one. As tired as I am, Lou, this has been fun. Maybe we can plan out a few of them, so we can go to one every couple of months. That way we'll be able to draw in more interest."

Blinking, I stared at her. "One convention every two months?" I shook my head. "No, I don't think I can do that."

"Give it time. It's not a decision we should make right now, because we're both exhausted, but after this is over, we should talk about it."

Even though I was certain there was no chance of me going to a convention every couple of months, I knew better than to argue then. "Okay."

Laying in the bed in the hotel room Katie got for me I wished I could sleep. I was exhausted, but it apparently wasn't enough to stop my mind. Katie had plans for Iron Phoenix. She obviously wanted to put a lot of time into it, to build it up into what she saw it, which involved regular conventions.

The convention was enjoyable. Even though I was more tired than I thought I'd ever been before I liked being there. At the same time, I couldn't imagine myself doing a lot of them when it was time, I could be working on other things. I sighed, closing my eyes, wondering if it was something Cole might have suggested if he actually cared about the work I was doing.

My phone rang. Reaching out a hand, certain there was only one person who'd be calling me so late, I pressed the button to tell it to shut up. I didn't want to talk to Cole right then. If it was anything truly important, he could leave a message, although I honestly doubted it was. He probably just wanted to make himself feel better by hearing my voice.

Hearing his voice wouldn't make me feel anything other than annoyed, so it was better not to answer. Sighing, I rolled onto my side, knowing I needed to sleep because we were going to have another long day. The phone rang again. Putting my hand out, telling myself I was going to turn it off if Cole didn't have a good reason for calling me at stupid o'clock.

"What do you want?"

Silence followed my question. "I thought you'd still be up, considering how busy you were today."

"Are you stalking me?"

"No, I'm not. One of my investors has a teenage daughter who went to the convention today. She returned home excited that you had willingly signed the art you were selling, and he called me to tell me about it. They like to keep track of you, to see what you're doing, although that was pure luck."

"I'm glad she appreciated it." I sat up. "Why did you call me?"

"Honestly, I wanted to check in to make sure you were still alive."

"One day at a convention isn't going to kill me. Two, however, might be a very different situation." I shook my head. "You don't need to check on me. I knew what I was getting into."

"Did you?"

"Mostly."

He laughed. "Which means you have no idea what you were signing up for, and you did it because Katie thought it would be a good idea."

"We both thought it would be a good idea. The convention has been enjoyable, even though it's exhausting." I bit down on my bottom lip. "This isn't something I'm certain I would have done if I knew how much energy it took, but I'm not going to say it was a mistake."

"How are things going with Katie?"

"Cole…"

"Yeah, I know I shouldn't ask, but I'm still interested in what you're doing."

"If only you were interested when we were married."

Even though I shouldn't have, I hung up on him, hoping it would keep him from calling me again because I didn't want to talk to him. For a few seconds I sat there with my phone in my hand, waiting to see what would happen. Instead of a call, I got a text. 'I'm sorry.'

Blinking back tears, not wanting to cry over Cole again, I lay back down, unable to keep myself from thinking what it would be like to do a convention with him. Would the two of us have shared the task of signing things, even though he'd not had anything to do with the creation of the games? It was unlikely he'd have known anything about the pins, but we could have learned together, the way we had done before.

A tear trickled down my cheek. I scrubbed it away, pulling the covers tighter around me, my emotions once again a mess. Why was it that he always seemed to call me when I was thinking about him? I shook my head at myself. That wasn't actually true, and it was obvious he was going to call me when I was thinking about him when I thought about him almost all the time. Breathing in deeply, closing my eyes, I tried to settle my emotions, not wanting to think about him anymore.

CHAPTER-12

Cole watched me from a slight distance away. I could see him every so often, at points when the crowd thinned slightly, and I took a moment when it seemed as quiet as it was going to get to slip out from behind the stall. From the way he moved away I didn't think he'd thought about what I might do when I saw him.

"Don't you have work to do?"

"Probably, but I felt like I needed to apologise properly. When I got here, I realised it was an apology I was giving you for me, and not for you." He sighed. "I am sorry, Lou. I wish I could have made better choices." He glanced at the stall. "What you've done is amazing. The games…" He breathed it in deeply. "I played one, for the first time, and I understand why this has happened."

"Now you understand." I shook my head. "After all this time."

"Yeah, I know. I'm an idiot."

"We both are, in some ways." I sighed. "We'll be done about nine, if you're free then."

He stared at me for a moment. "You're willing to spend some time together?"

"If that's something you want." I ran my tongue over my dry lips. "I don't know what I want right now, but I still think about you all the time. Maybe I do need some kind of closure."

"Maybe we both do. I should have talked to you before, and worked through some of this, rather than shutting you out." Cole raked a hand through his hair. "I remember doing that when we first got together because I didn't know how to talk to you. We worked through it together, you told me how important it was for the two of us to communicate, so it's not a surprise that the time finally came when you made the decision that you couldn't live with it anymore.

"Especially as we were also meant to be business partners. I failed you in multiple ways, and I don't deserve a chance to talk to you. I honestly don't know why I thought coming here was a good idea. You deserved better." He put a hand on my shoulder, and I could feel his warmth coming through my shirt. "I'll be here at nine. If you change your mind then let me know."

Before I could say anything more, he was gone. Heading back to the stall I found a few people waiting for me to sign things, which was a good distraction. As I took the time to sign multiple pictures for people who loved the worlds, I'd created I felt Katie's eyes on me. Ignoring her probably wasn't the best decision to make, but I also couldn't bring myself to talk to her about Cole. I knew what she thought about him. Telling her I'd made the decision I was going to spend some time with him probably wouldn't go well.

***

Lunch seemed to be one of the quieter times. We both sat together, eating some kind of pasta we'd bought from the hall, and I knew she was waiting for the right moment to bring up what happened with Cole. Every so often she glanced at me. I focused on my food rather than her because I was hungrier than I think I'd ever been.

"I understand."

"You understand what?"

"Spending time with Cole." I looked at her then, her eyes meeting mine. "You thought I was going to judge you because I wouldn't be making the same choices as you." She shook her head. "Lou, I'm not that kind of person. I might not understand how you feel, as I've never been there, but I don't think it's my place to stop you from doing something you believe is right.

"Even though love isn't enough to hold a relationship together it doesn't mean there's nothing between the two of you. I know how much Cole still means to you. Maybe it's not love. Maybe it's the last light of love, slowly fading. Either way, you need to make your choices. If you want to see where things can go then you can see where things can go."

"That's not going to happen. I think it is the last light of love, Katie, and I want to say goodbye. His emotions kept him from talking to me when our relationship came to a legal end, so this is my chance to say what I need to say." I shrugged. "When I said I didn't want to go back I meant it. I'm not going to get back into a relationship with him, or start working with Kingston again."

"I know." She put her hand on my arm. "Whatever decision you make - it has to be yours. I'm not going to say anything about it, other than to tell you that you have my support. You always will."

Nodding, I looked over at the person who'd been browsing, and he looked back at me, his eyes meeting mine. "Can you sign these?"

"Of course." I stood, putting the pasta down on my chair. "Did you want anything specific on it?"

"Actually, if you can, they're for my son. He's been into your games for a long time, and I was hoping to bring him, but this was his mom's weekend, something she wasn't willing to give up. Even though he can't be here I thought I could get him something from one of his favourite games."

Looking at the pictures, seeing which game they were from, I bit down on my bottom lip. "His name?"

"Will."

Signing the pictures to Will, I also started to gather the full collection of pins for the game, which I put into one of the bags. "Give this to him. Tell him this is one of my favourites too."

The guy looked at the bag of pins. "Are you sure?"

"I'm sure."

As he took them, handing over the money for the pictures, I could see the emotion in his eyes. "Thank you so much. He's going to be so happy with this."

Before he could break down, something I was certain was about to happen, he walked away, and I looked back at Katie. "I'll pay for them."

"No, you won't. I'd have done the same thing." She gestured for me to sit down. "Sometimes we're allowed to do nice things for the people who come to buy from us. You could hear the love in his voice, and I think Will will be happy to get a full set of pins. Maybe next time we're here we'll actually see him."

"Maybe." I picked up my pasta again. "You meant it when you were talking about a convention every two months, didn't you?"

"Connecting with people is something I love to do. Seeing them all sharing their love for the games you've created with us, and each other... it's worth the energy. If you can't do every other month then maybe you can do every four, and I can do every two. We can still sell signed pictures, but some will be sold by you, and some will be sold by me."

"We'll see how things go." I looked at the table once more, a small group was beginning to gather. "Your turn."

Laughing, Katie stood, stepping over to see what they wanted. She'd already finished eating, and I took the time I needed to finish eating before I joined her, tossing the pots in the bin as I passed them. The numbers were growing once more and our short break was over, so both of us were needed.

* * *

Cole was at the door when we left, his eyes meeting with mine for a moment. "You want to get something to eat?"

Nodding, I glanced at Katie. "I'll see you in the morning."

"Are you going to be, okay?"

"Of course. I'll order room service, and sleep." She smiled, and then looked at Cole. "Make sure she gets to bed at a reasonable time."

"Will do."

I watched her walk away, before turning back to Cole, who led me down the street. The good thing about where they'd set up the convention was that there were plenty of places to eat. Did he have a plan for food? I hoped he had a plan, because I didn't want to have to think.

Fortunately, he led me straight to the nearest Indian. "Oh, this is great."

"Yeah, I thought you'd like this one." He opened the door, stepping to one side to let me in. "I even ordered already. I told them you were up at the convention, and it seems they have a number of people who come in to order early for people who are working there until late, so it should be close to being ready."

Biting down on my lip, to keep myself from saying anything that might make him unhappy, I followed him to the table. Sitting down I found there was also a drink, which looked like it was lemonade, and I took a sip, grateful for the cold fizziness. "Thank you." I breathed in deeply. "I do appreciate this, but I can't help wondering why you're being so thoughtful."

"To apologise in actions. I feel like this might be one of the last times we see each other. We're both living different lives now, and I don't want to keep dragging us both back into the past because it's not good for either of us as we attempt to move forward. I just…" He shrugged. "No matter what I wanted you to know I did still care about you, something I know I failed to show you before everything changed.

"What I feel now, more than anything, is love for you. You did everything you could to help me, and I know you did. I brought up the Virtual School, asked you for help, and you did far more than I could have believed was possible. When I said before I was jealous, I was being honest with you for the first time in far too long."

He fell silent as the food was placed in front of each of us. "Thank you." He smiled at the waiter. "I appreciate you doing this for us."

"You're welcome." The waiter looked at me. "I hope you enjoy it. My daughter met you earlier, and she said you were lovely to her. Someone like you makes the convention far more enjoyable."

"I'm glad she had a good experience."

The waiter left us, and I picked up my fork. "From the sounds of things, you're making a lot of people happy."

"They deserve it because they put in the effort to come to us." I shrugged. "You said you were honest with me before."

Nodding, he picked up his fork, stabbing it into a piece of meat. "I'd kept so much from you because I was scared, you'd leave if I was. Only I ended up making you feel so uncomfortable, my disconnection from you to much for you to live with, and you left anyway."

"Did you care more about our marriage or the company?"

Cole shook his head." I don't know. I wish I had an answer for you, Lou, but so much of this has been worked through since you left, which is why I was able to have a conversation with you about it now." He ate another piece of meat. "It's still not the right time, because I don't have all the answers you deserve. I just... I know you want me to leave you alone. If I was in your position, I'd feel the same way."

"We both need a chance to move on, like you said. That's not something we can do if you're still clinging to the relationship we once had. I want a chance to live my life the way I think is right."

CHAPTER-13

e stopped outside the hotel, Cole by my side, and I looked at him. "I guess this is goodbye."

He nodded. "Yeah, I guess it is." There was emotion in his eyes I couldn't read. "I love you, Lou." He kissed my cheek. "Be happy."

"You too." I gave him one last hug. "One day we might be able to be friends, but there's a lot for both of us to work through before that can happen."

Stepping back, his eyes met mine, and he moved into the darkness a little more than before. "We do. Good luck. I hope Iron Phoenix works out exactly the way you dream."

I wished there was something more to say, but it was done. Our relationship was over. The divorce had been finalised weeks before, and this was nothing more than a last goodbye because we both needed it. Without saying anything more I stepped into the hotel, knowing I was making the best choice I could.

As I headed up to my room, I finally felt the weight of it off my shoulders. It seemed I did need that closure, even though I hadn't known that for certain until it happened. Now I can move forward with my life. Moving forward did mean spending another day at the convention, and then I could make a decision about what it was I was going to do next with Iron Phoenix.

Entering the room, breathing in deeply, I dropped into the bed. After far too long I was myself again. Part of me, it seemed, had still been entwined with Cole, and Kingston Interactive. Now I have it back. Maybe I'd let myself take it back because I'd linked my life to his so much, and being able to say goodbye helped.

Next thing I knew I woke up, still in my clothes from the night before. Pulling my phone out of my pocket I looked at the time. It was almost 3 a.m. Well, I obviously needed the sleep. Standing, I stripped out of my day clothes, finding my pyjamas. My alarm would be going off far sooner than I wanted it to but I could get a little more sleep.

Curling up under the covers, I must have crashed out straight away because the next thing I knew the alarm was going off. Part of me wanted to snooze it, but I didn't and dragged myself out of the bed to shower. I needed to smell good if I was going to be selling things to people.

Fortunately, the shower did help me wake up a little. Wrapping myself in towels, and checked the time once more, I knew I needed to move faster, and I headed into my room to get dressed. Leaving Katie to get set up alone wasn't something I wanted to do, so I threw on some clean clothes, including an Iron Phoenix t-shirt, before making my way down to the lobby, where she was waiting for me.

***

Being able to pack everything up, knowing we weren't going back, was a relief in ways I couldn't put into words. It had been three very long days. We'd sold almost everything we had with us, which was exactly what we hoped to do. Making our way to Katie's car, with the flattened boxes, I unlocked it and slipped them into the back seat.

Katie followed behind me, carrying the few things we would need to sell elsewhere. "Do you think we should buy more Iron Phoenix merchandise?"

"That's a decision I want to wait to make." I glanced at her. "I'm not certain what steps I want to take next, but I do feel like I'm at the point where I can make them now." Slowly, I ran my tongue over my bottom lip, hoping she'd understand. "Last night was good. I feel like whatever part of me was still connected to Cole and Kingston is mine again." I shook my head. "I don't even know what that means."

"Oh, I do." Katie smiled, taking the keys from me, and going round to the driver's side. "After working with Dad, I completely understand what it feels like when a part of you has been left behind." She gestured for me to get in, so I did. "You put so much energy, and love, into what you were doing, and it's hard to let it go. Being able to say goodbye, I think, does help. You got that last night."

"Yeah, I did, and we both made the decision together that there was no going back. We need to move forward. It might be as friends, in the future, but for now that's not a possibility."

Nodding, Katie started the car. "An understandable decision."

As we drove in silence alone on the street, I felt like I should say something more, but it was kind of nice after the noise of the day. If Katie wanted to break it, I wouldn't have stopped her. From the way she didn't though it seemed that she too appreciated the lack of sound as much as I did.,

Reaching Patterson's car park, Katie pulled into her normal spot, and I climbed out of the car, planning on helping. "Go home, Lou. I've got this." She pulled me into a hug. "I'll see you in a couple of days. Then we might be able to talk about what your plans are, and we can go from there."

"You're sure?"

"I'm sure." She stepped back. "You've done a lot of work the last few days, and I want you to get home safely tonight."

"Okay, then I'll see you on Thursday."

Heading over to my own car, thinking about what I did want to do, I glanced back over to see Katie taking the boxes into the building. Sighing, I raked a hand through my hair. I knew what she'd said, but I still felt like I should have done more, after having spent three days signing what felt like hundreds of pictures.

***

Being home was nice. It was late, and I was tired, so I should have gone to bed, but instead I found myself sitting in my office. Pulling a notebook toward me, I started to write. I remembered doing something similar before when we were first starting out with Kingston Interactive, trying to work through my thoughts.

The only thing I was certain of was that I wanted to keep making games. I'd done too much to stop, and the convention taught me one important thing - people loved what I did. They cared about the characters I'd created. Sighing, I raked a hand through my hair. I didn't feel like there was a right option. Working alone felt right, but at the same time, it meant I never got time out.

Working with Katie gave me a chance to do different things. I was still in charge of the creative aspects, and I could start working with other people. Like Paul. Glancing at the time, to find it was well past midnight, I knew it wasn't a time I could call him. After Cole shut down my plans to work with Patterson's originally, I told Paul we might not be able to move forward with the plans he had.

It was possible I could bring him in, to work with Iron Phoenix. I knew he had his own ideas, and it was something Katie would appreciate because she wanted to grow the division. Biting down on my lip, I raked a hand through my hair again, wondering it if might be better for

Paul became a part of Patterson's, while I did something else.

Did I really want to work alone? I did, and I didn't. Working with Katie was similar to working alone. She didn't want to take control, but she did want to work with other developers. Slowly, nodding, I thought I had my decision made, as long as Katie was okay with it. I had no reason to think she wouldn't be.

A complicated decision made I headed to bed. I'd call Paul in the morning, see if he still wanted to work with a larger company, and then we could go from there. I might also call Katie, although that was also a conversation, I could have another day. She said Thursday, when we'd both had a chance to rest after three days at a very busy convention.

Yawning, I lay down, my bed feeling far more comfortable than the hotel bed was. I set an alarm on my phone, so I wasn't up stupid late, before closing my eyes. Of course, the exhaustion wasn't enough for me to sleep. I kept my eyes closed, breathing slowly, remembering how to put myself to sleep, something I'd failed at more than once. Slowly, sleep crept over me. I rolled onto my side, pulling the covers up, warm, comfortable, and certain of my path.

"Lou?"

"Hi, Paul. I know it's been a very long time." I raked a hand through my hair, trying to find the right words. "Calling you is something I should have done months ago." I bit down on my bottom lip. "Things have been... complicated."

"There are some things I saw. You've started working with Patterson's."

Nodding, I smiled. "Yeah, Katie and I have a provisional contract, which is part of the reason I didn't want to bring anything up until I was more certain of what I wanted to do next. There was a chance I might not have stayed because I didn't know if I was comfortable working at Patterson's, but I believe I will be, once I've had another conversation with Katie.

"With that decision made I wanted to ask if you had any plans. After how I had to change things before, I honestly wouldn't be surprised if you didn't want to work with me, but..." I sighed. "I was doing what I thought was best, knowing things with Cole were... well, it's hard to put into words."

"Obviously things didn't work out."

"Cole and I divorced. The business... in the end it came between us, and it's been hard. Moving on is more complicated than I could have ever imagined. Last night we had a long conversation where we worked through some things, and it's going to be easier for both of us to build a different life. One without the other."

"I'm sorry, Lou. I did hope you'd be able to make things work." He was silent for a few seconds. "Let me have a couple of days, and then we can talk through some options. Creating games is something I've not done much since then. I can look through what I had, and then make some decisions for myself. I do understand why you made the choices you did. Bringing me into Kingston Interactive wouldn't have been the right choice."

"Okay, I'll wait to hear from you. If you don't want to get involved, I do understand, but Iron Phoenix will exist even if I'm not there. Katie really wants to start building it up more, because it's something she loves, more than I realised until we started working together, and she'd keep you on no matter what happens."

"That's good to hear. Thank you for calling. I do appreciate it." I could hear the smile in his voice. "I'll call you."

"Bye, Paul."

"Bye, Lou."

He hung up, and I breathed a sigh of relief. That was one task done. Next, I needed to talk to Katie, but that was a job for another day. I headed into the office, going through some of the plans I had for the next game I was working on, planning out a series of dialogue that seemed to not be working quite the way I wanted it to while I was writing on the computer. I did find that writing things by hand did help sometimes.

CHAPTER-14

Katie nodded. "I'm happy with that." She studied me. "Okay, so, you are Iron Phoenix, and I'll work out a different name for Patterson's game division." Her eyes met with mine. "That's what you want, right?"

"As long as it does work. The last thing I want to do is make things more complicated, but I want to have a certain amount of control. It's…" I shook my head. "Working with Cole, I gave up that control because Kingston was always more his. I know Patterson's is yours, and I'm working with you, so you do have a veto if I want to bring anything out you don't feel fits Patterson's brand. At the same time, I just… I don't know quite how to put it into words."

"The contract we signed before already states you have total control over your IP, and we can include Iron Phoenix in that." She put her hand on mine. "You're my friend, Lou, so the last thing I want to do is make you feel uncomfortable when you're working with me. The worlds of Iron Phoenix are something I love, and I will do whatever I can to make things easier for you."

"I know, and you've said that before. Going round in circles isn't something I like doing, but things have been so complicated recently. Seeing Cole was a reminder of how easy it was for me to give up parts of myself. That's something I don't want to do again."

"Of course, you don't." She squeezed my hand. "I've said before you have my support, whatever choice you make, but I have to admit I'm glad I get to be a part of this."

"So am I." I smiled. "Yesterday I got in contact with an old colleague of mine. I think I mentioned him when we were first talking about you becoming an investor for Kingston. When things started becoming more complicated with Cole, and Kingston, I made the decision it was best not to drag Paul into it, so I had to tell him it wouldn't work.

"When I talked to him, I told him there was going to be a gaming division here irrespective of the choice I made, but I believed I was going to be staying. He's someone I think you'd like to work with, although he does still need to make a decision himself because he isn't this is still someone, he wants to do."

"Okay, well, when do you think we can talk it through together? Then if he does want to join us, we can work through what his plans are, so we can have a mixed release schedule. I am also in contact with a couple of other potential developers, to see if they want to join us. A couple of them said they wanted to speak to you before they made a decision."

***

Katie sat beside me, the two of us conversing with one of the developers she hoped would join the division, which we had yet to name."The plan is for each developer to control their own IP. I don't want control over what you're making, but I do want to support different developers I like. You're one of those developers."

I nodded. "The contract I signed with Patterson's stated that. I have full control over my IP, and Katie's a wonderful person to talk to if you have any problems. She's willing to work with us, along with supporting us to move forward with what we're doing, without having to lose any control over the worlds we've been working to create.

"As a developer myself, I've appreciated the support I get from Katie. We've talked through a lot of my issues, which come from working in a more complicated situation before, and she's incredibly patient with me having long circular conversations. The two of us also spent a few days at a convention recently, which is something she had plans to do more of in the future."

"Yes, I do, for the division. The first one only had Iron Phoenix there, but if you were to join us, I'd help work on a new collection of merchandise. You're welcome to come with me, and I'll pay for everyone, or you can send me off alone because this doesn't only help to build the division, it also helps to build up awareness of Patterson's.

"The more developers we have working with us the easier it will be for us to bring money into the company. From there the money will go into supporting the developers. My plan, in the end, is to have a group of five or six developers all working for the gaming division of Patterson's, but I might have more if there's anyone you can suggest we talk to."

Slowly, the developer nodded, looking between us. "There are a couple of devs I can think of. I don't know whether they would be willing to join you, but we've all been looking for someone to support us. Being a developer without support is hard."

"Join Patterson's, and you won't have that problem anymore." Katie smiled. "We have a six-month provisional contract, so if you find you aren't happy you can leave, without there being any issues. I don't want anyone to feel like they're trapped here."

He raked a hand through his hair. "Give me a couple of days to think about it, and I'll get back to you."

"Of course. Take as long as you need. The offer's not going away. Please give my contact details to anyone you think might want to work with me."

Silence followed as he hung up the call, and I looked at Katie. "Is that what you were hoping for?"

"Being able to talk to a developer working with me will make it easier for them to decide what their next steps are. I think it went well, and there's a chance he might be able to bring others in."

***

"Hi, Paul."

"Lou." There was a moment of silence. "I've gone through everything I did before, wondering if it was what I wanted, and I felt the same excitement I did before. Taking a step away from it was something I did due to lack of time, more than anything else because I needed to work, otherwise, I wouldn't have a roof over my head.

"You said I'd have the support of Patterson's gaming division if I was willing to join with you, so I wanted to know if that was still available. I'm not as far forward with the work as I'd like to be, but it shouldn't take me too much longer to get it finished. I just... I can't do it without the money."

Nodding, I stepped over to where Katie was. "How about you talk to the woman who's leading the division, and then you can make a choice as to what it is you want to do?" I held the phone out to her. "This is my old colleague, Paul. He was thinking of joining us, but he wanted to talk to you."

Smiling, Katie took the phone from me, pressing it to her ear. "Hi, Paul. I'm Katie. Lou said you were hoping to join us."

Knowing what Katie was going to say because I'd heard it multiple times throughout the day, I stepped away from the conversation. There was no need for me to be there to hear it all again. Sitting at the desk she'd set up with me for the days I was working at Patterson's, I started going through the dialogue again, wondering if I simply needed to try again with it. Unfortunately, there were times when something didn't work quite the way I hoped it would. This might be one of them.

Putting the first sentence on a new page, trying not to think about the dialogue I remembered writing before, I tried to come up with something that flowed the way I wanted it to. Every word felt like it was wrong. Was I starting in the wrong place? Sighing, I raked a hand through my hair, trying to work out what the best next step was.

Before I could make a decision, Katie was there, passing me my phone back. "Paul?"

"Katie invited me to come to Patterson's to have a conversation with the two of you this afternoon."

"Okay, that's good." I looked at Katie, and she gave me a thumbs up before stepping away. She obviously thought he was someone we wanted with us. "Make sure you bring some of your work with you. We're going to see it, although I think I remember it from before." I smiled. "You were good, Paul, and I'm glad you made this decision. I'm looking forward to seeing you later."

"I'm looking forward to seeing you too."

As Paul walked into the office, he gave me a smile. I smiled back, going over to join Katie, who looked happy to have another potential developer in the office. "It's a pleasure to meet you, Paul. I believe you were going to show me what you have so far." She gestured for him to sit down. "You took a step back when it became obvious you weren't going to be able to work with Kingston Interactive?"

"Yeah, I did." He took the offered seat. "Originally, Lou and I were working out plans, but when Cole made it obvious, he wasn't willing to work with you because you wanted to work with Lou rather than Kingston, she said it was probably best to wait. At the time I wasn't entirely certain why she thought that. Now I know what happened I understand the wariness. Had I been in her position I would have made the same decision.

"Working on games wasn't something I knew I wanted to do until we started working together. Lou and I became friends as we learnt how to code games together, so it made sense to work with her. Now that I have another chance to do that and I'm certain it's the path I want to take, but, as I'm sure you know, it's not an easy thing to do."

"How much have you done recently?"

"Going back through the games I'd been working on is something I did after Lou called. Seeing them again, after stepping away, was like being back where I was supposed to be, and I've been doing some work over the last couple of days. I feel like I can get the first game finished off in the next couple of months. It was close to being ready before."

"First, I want to play a demo. I know the games I like, and I'm choosing the developers I work with based on that, but as Lou recommended you, I have no reason to think that will be a problem." Katie smiled. "After I've played the demo, we can talk about a contract."

Nodding, Paul pulled a USB stick out of his pocket. "This is what I have of the game. It's got most of the world in place, and about 40 hours of gameplay, depending on what you do. I still want to work on some more side quests, but I don't think too much is missing."

"This is good." Katie looked at me. "How are you feeling, Lou?"

"I played the game before when we were working through things together, and I'm certain it's going to be good." Paul's eyes met mine, making it possible for me to see how grateful he was. "I think you'll enjoy it, Kate."

"Okay, how about you hang around while I spend half an hour playing the game. Lou can take you to look around the building, meet some people, and when you come back, I should have a decision for you."

"Great. Thank you for giving me the time."

Smiling, I stepped around the desk. "Come on then. This is a good chance for us to catch up."

www.ingramcontent.com/pod-product-compliance
Lightning Source LLC
LaVergne TN
LVHW061553070526
838199LV00077B/7034